SHORT CUTS

INTRODUCTIONS TO FILM STUDIES

COSTUME AND CINEMA

DRESS CODES IN POPULAR FILM

SARAH STREET

WALLFLOWER

LONDON and NEW YORK

A Wallflower Paperback

First published in Great Britain in 2001 by Wallflower Press
5 Pond Street, Hampstead, London NW3 2PN
www.wallflowerpress.co.uk

A catalogue record for this book is available from the British Library

ISBN 1 903364 18 3

Book Design by Rob Bowden Design

Printed in Great Britain by Biddles Limited, Guildford and King's Lynn

CONTENTS

LIST OF ILLUSTRATIONS

ACKNOWLEDGEMENTS

Thanks go to Sue Simkin for reading drafts of all the chapters and to Simon Jones for his comments on *The Talented Mr Ripley* and *The Matrix*. The readers for Wallflower Press also provided some valuable comments. The stills were located in the Kobal Archive and I thank them once again for their efficiency and enthusiasm for the project. Finally, I would like to thank Wallflower Press for inviting me to write this 'short' book and giving me the opportunity to look at film costume once more.

INTRODUCTION: CHANGING TEXTS

The study of costume and cinema is only just beginning to be recognised as a legitimate and fruitful subject area. As Pam Cook notes: 'The marginalisation of costume design by film theorists is marked enough to be diagnosed as a symptom' (1996: 41). The possible reasons for the relative scarcity of sustained analyses of film costume have been suggested by Pamela Church Gibson: the assumption, held by many academics, that fashion is a frivolous, feminine field; the suspicion that fashion is merely an expression of capitalist commodity fetishism and the opinion, held by some feminists, that fashion is one of the primary ways in which women are trapped into gratifying the male gaze (1998: 36). Recent scholarship has challenged this negative view, opening up the subject to fresh approaches by suggesting the ways in which film costume can be linked to wider debates about film form, the meaning and function of mise-en-scène, the role of the costume designer, the complex ways in which film costumes are 'read' as intertexts and, finally, the impact of such representations on audiences in their everyday behaviours and appearances.

A wide-ranging literature on fashion and the fashion industry has produced significant and thought-provoking insights into the relationship between clothes and the body, and also between fashion and society (for a summary see Entwistle 2000: 40-77 and bibliographic references for further reading at the end of this book). It is not the project of this book to present a detailed survey of fashion history and theory. It is nevertheless important to refer to key ideas that, while not developed with film in mind, are relevant to the use of costume in films, particularly ideas about fashion operating as a 'system'. Anthropologists, sociologists and psychologists, for example, have made serious attempts to theorize distinctions between 'dress' and 'fashion'. As Entwistle explains, while anthropologists have been preoccupied with studying 'dress' as a general activity, sociologists and psychologists have identified 'fashion' as 'a system of dress characterised by an internal logic of regular and systematic change' (Entwistle 2000: 44). Indeed, fashion has been analysed by some theorists as a 'problem' for the western world, as an effect of monopoly capitalism with competition as the key dynamic for change (see, for example, Veblen 1899/1953, Simmel 1904/1957, 1971 and Tseëlon 1992). This literature offers interesting perspectives, particularly the assumption that dress can be related to status and to social class. As we shall see, film costuming frequently operates as a 'system' governed by complex influences that relate to notions of realism, performance, gender, status and power.

From a psychoanalytic perspective, and also relevant to the study of films, the work of John Flügel (1930: 20-22) is instructive in its identification of an ambivalent attitude towards clothes that originates in the contradictory impulses of exhibitionism and modesty. For Flügel, clothes are an extension of the 'bodily self' that is less ashamed when clothed: clothes can be used as protection, as a sort of armour that conceals vulnerability but also as display, often of a sexual nature. This intriguing relationship between clothes and the body has been a key area of debate, encompassing questions of gender. While Flügel's work concentrated on the psychic impulses behind dress and fashion, he shared with James Laver (1969) a concern with gender differences and fashion, differences that can be seen to resonate in film costumes. Both theorists claimed that women were more narcissistic than men and Laver in particular identified women's use of clothing as primarily concerned with attracting sexual attention from men (1969: 14). In classical Hollywood cinema, great emphasis was placed on female costuming as intimately related to sexual attractiveness and, in Laura Mulvey's (1975) terms, as gratifying the male gaze. As a reaction to this, subsequent feminist scholarship sought to revise the view that the gaze was male (see Stacey 1994: 19-48) and also that fashion was an inherently frivolous preoccupation.

Although not directly concerned with film, Elizabeth Wilson's book, *Adorned In Dreams* (1985), contributed to a feminist re-appropriation of fashion. Wilson's rejection of feminist austerity (represented by writers such as Simone de Beauvoir (1949)) suggested new ways of thinking about fashion as a focus of liberation, a site of opposition and a complex signifier of gender and sexuality. Above all, she argued that the ambiguities surrounding dress provide a crucial link with conceptions of the body: 'If the body with its open orifices is itself dangerously ambiguous, then dress, which is an extension of the body yet not quite part of it, not only links that body to the social world, but also more clearly separates the two. Dress is the frontier between the self and the not-self' (1985: 3). Wilson's observation about the duality represented by dress in everyday life raises questions about the extent to which screen representations explore such ambiguity: how do film fashions function, and relate to characterization, narrative, images of the body and audience response?

Annette Kuhn has argued that dress has a crucial performative function, as a masquerade that can be used to 'reconstruct the wearer's self' (1985: 52). Similarly, postmodern theorist Judith Butler (1990) notes how performance is a key element of gender as a socially-constructed and hence mutable category, as opposed to sex which is biologically determined. Consequently, costume plays a key role in the construction of gender codes and expectations. Indeed, the vast literature on masculinity has contributed to a revision of the binarist view that fashion is purely a female concern. As Stella Bruzzi (1997: 67-94) has demonstrated in relation to the gangster film, male costumes are revealing about the sartorial representation of status, money and style. Also, as Susan Jeffords (1989) and Lynne Segal (1990) have argued, male costuming is often used as a disguise for vulnerability or an attempt to negotiate the incomplete and contradictory impulses between masculine and feminine that constitute 'masculinity'. In particular, the prominence of the 'new man' in recent years has been accompanied by a range of fashions that challenge established conventions of men's clothing that were concerned with 'the display of restraint in a disciplined body' (Craik 1994: 203). Here, the under-researched area of male costuming will be discussed further in the chapters on *Plein Soleil* and *The Talented Mr Ripley* and on *The Matrix*.

The literature on film costume can be divided between the 'coffee table' books that chronicle the work of fashion designers in the film industry (see Chierichetti 1976; Engelmeier 1997), and books concerned with analysing the function of costume in film texts. The former are useful in tracing the relationship between Hollywood and the fashion industry, celebrating couturier designs as well as the work of studio costume designers such as Edith Head. Costume was intimately related to the 'look' of a particular studio and star, as well as to the mechanics of popular genre production. Hollywood has dominated this particular type of publication, the emphasis being on glamour and spectacle, as demonstrated by the books' lavish production, illustrated with many photographs of celebrated costumes. While they are useful, attractive, and are aimed at a wider audience than academic books, they seldom deal with how costume actually works in a film text and may well, unwittingly, have contributed to the idea that film costume is not worthy of serious analysis.

By contrast, the literature on film texts has largely been concerned with the ability of film costume to support or transcend the demands of film narrative: to what extent can film costume be said to articulate a language of its own, capable of offering alternative interpretations from the main thrust of the plot and characterization? Roland Barthes (1983) applied a *semiotic** ('terms indicated with an asterisk are defined in the

Glossary) approach to studying the 'fashion system' by looking closely at fashion magazines to determine their meaning at any given time; film scholars have also studied the system governing the function of film costume. But unlike the 'frozen' text of a magazine, the study of film fashions invites consideration of their role in the overall narrative.

The issue of narrative has been raised by Jane Gaines and Charlotte Herzog in *Fabrications* (1990), an influential collection of essays which developed some of Wilson's ideas with reference to film. Gaines argues that for the majority of Hollywood cinema, costume has been 'reined in' to serve narrative: 'Narrative realism dictates that costume be curtailed by conventional dress codes; continuity requires that it be monitored for the telltale continuity error; economy requires that it reinforce causality' (1990: 196). On the other hand, Gaines concedes that in film melodramas costume can perform a more assertive, 'excessive' function, but in the most part it tends to be related to the demands of plot and story. In terms of expressing a character's emotional core, costume, she argues, can be empathetic: 'Richness of feeling deserves enriched texture, and velvet, wool jersey, chiffon, satin, bugle-beading, or sable are often used on the bodies of these heroines' (208). In the same collection, however, several essays point the way to a more dynamic role for costume in film, for example, in the case of the spectacle of films which feature fashion shows (see Herzog 1990: 134-59).

Stella Bruzzi's book *Undressing Cinema* (1997) extends this argument further, proposing that some film costumes function as 'iconic clothes': 'spectacular interventions that interfere with the scenes in which they appear and impose themselves onto the character they adorn' (1997: xv). Furthermore, she makes the case that couturier designs* in particular exercise this function, frequently disrupting the narrative by creating an authorial statement by the couturier for the spectatorial gaze, 'to be admired or acknowledged in spite of the general trajectory of the film' (34). In *Kika* (Pedro Almodóvar, 1993), Jean-Paul Gaultier's vamp and robot costumes for Andrea (Victoria Abril) are therefore 'pure spectacle' (13). Bruzzi's book also examines male film costuming, as well as raising interesting questions about race and costume and also issues of androgyny. Above all, she extends the boundaries of film costume analysis, correctly recognizing its function as a 'discourse not wholly dependent on the structures of narrative and character for signification' (xvi). Drawing on Bruzzi's model, Gaines (in Bruzzi and Church Gibson 2000: 159-177) has examined the role of one particularly spectacular dress 'that consumes our seeing' (167) designed by Adrian for *Madam Satan* (Cecil B. DeMille 1930).

As well as this important work on the relationship between costume and film narrative, several film scholars have concentrated on the symbolic role which costumes might adopt within a particular narrative construction. Studies of the film noir genre have drawn attention to the function of costume in texts which can be read from a psychoanalytic perspective. The image of the *femme fatale**, for example, can be taken to embody male castration anxiety, as her costumes are fetishised to allay male fears about 'lack' (see Hayward 2000: 446-8). In particular, Sue Harper and Pam Cook's studies of British Gainsborough melodramas relate costume to sexual symbolism. Harper's analysis of *The Wicked Lady* (Leslie Arliss, 1945) equates Margaret Lockwood's first appearance as Barbara, the transgressive heroine, wearing a velvet fur-trimmed, silk-lined coat, with vulval symbolism (1994: 130). Cook's discussion of *Madonna of the Seven Moons* (Arthur Crabtree, 1944) shows how the central character's 'split personality' – that of an upper-class woman and a hedonistic gypsy – is represented through costume as a complex signifier of associated emotional and sexual themes (1996: 93). In this way, film costumes can exceed the demands of the plot or historical accuracy, conveying a sophisticated address which can be said to constitute a 'language' of its own, offering an alternative discourse from that suggested by the 'preferred' reading. Following on from this proposition, Bruzzi's study of costume films proposes that restrictive and regulatory Victorian costumes can arouse desire in a *fetishistic** sense. In films such as *The Piano* (Jane Campion, 1993), which empower the female central character with access to 'the look' of sexual desire, the Freudian concept which is normally associated with men can be applied to a woman because 'both costume and the body appear linked in this film to a complex feminist displacement of the unconventionalised objectification of the women's form via *scopophilia** and fetishism' (Bruzzi 1997: 58). My work on costume and accessories in the films of Alfred Hitchcock has also pointed to the ways in which costume can be read as a complex system with symbolic meanings (1995-6: 23-37; 2000: 91-109). These debates about narrative and questions of symbolism will be returned to in the discussion of costume and *heritage** cinema in James Cameron's *Titanic* (1997).

As texts, films draw on complex codes of *verisimilitude** in order to convince and enthral their audiences. These will either accord with a notion of generic verisimilitude which presents costumes as part of a genre's iconography, for example gangster suits and hats, or with a notion of social verisimilitude which audiences equate with their own lived experience – costumes that convince as being 'realistic' or appropriate to a particular situation (see Neale 2000: 31-9). The understanding of character, for example, is particularly fascinating via a study of film costumes. If the audience has 'suspended disbelief', it is possible that there might be an 'imagined embodiment' in process whereby the audience imagines that the character has exercised a degree of individual agency when deciding what to wear, just as they experience in their own lives. 'Imagined' or 'assumed embodiment' might, therefore, be an integral aspect of our response to costume and characterization. It is important, therefore, to recognise that film costumes not only relate to the characters who wear them but also to the audiences who watch them. Jennifer Craik (1994) and Joanne Entwistle (2000) have suggested that the processes of 'lived experience' – how people use fashion in everyday life – must be central to analyses of dress and fashion in contemporary society: the challenge is how to incorporate this into the study of texts. A key area of scholarship in relation to film costumes has therefore been exploring their impact on audiences. Much of the literature on screen fashions has assumed a magical transference of stardom from screen to audience. As Melanie Hillmer has written:

> The clothes worn by immortal stars and long-forgotten starlets serve as a pattern for our dreams and nightmares, and for things of which we have not yet dreamed. When we take clothes out of context, we can slip into the role of Marlene, Humphrey, Audrey, James, speaking their sartorial language with our bodies. We are the copy, the variation, the improvisation, the parody. (1997: 12)

It appears to be the case that as far as Hollywood was concerned, audiences frequently adapted what they saw on screen for their own wardrobe. Sometimes this was a deliberate commercial strategy. Charles Eckert's influential study of commercial *tie-ins** between merchandise companies, department stores and screen fashions in Hollywood was the first sustained consideration of how in a commercial sense audiences were encouraged to emulate what they saw on screen (1990: 100-21). This did not however occur in a passive, simply exploitative manner. As Sarah Berry has demonstrated in her work on film fashions and female consumers in 1930s America, 'consumer fashion and film costume are potentially subversive because they encourage fantasies of self-transformation while drawing attention to the conventional basis of social types and categories' (2000: 185). The resulting 'style consciousness', facilitated by a range of clothes that were made in imitation of those worn by film stars on and off-screen, was therefore more than a direct result of 'top-down' aggressive merchandising. As Jackie Stacey has shown in her study of the impact of Hollywood cinema on British audiences, the adaptive processes at work involved 'bottom-up' creativity, requiring a considerable degree of individual choice in the emulation of screen fashions (1994: 126-75). Craik also points out that fashion is a 'process of acculturation' whereby styles popularised by films are utilized by means of 'selective borrowings' in everyday wear (1993: 16-17). The question of the impact of film costume on audiences will be raised in the case study of *Desperately Seeking Susan*, foregrounding some of the difficult methodological issues relating to the assessment of audience behaviours, in particular the extent to which film costumes influence imitation or 'embodiment' of what has been displayed on screen.

As well as being influenced by the above ideas on costume and cinema this book will develop the idea of 'adaptation' as a means of identifying films which use costume in interesting ways and which can be studied with reference to a method of comparative *intertextuality**. As will already be apparent, at a textual level film costumes engage with a complex and mutable process. To adapt something means to 'fit, adjust, modify, make suitable' and film costumes do exactly this: they conform to notions of realism but also need to employ notions of cinematic spectacle. Even though their designers are often at pains to point out the extent of historical research that has been undertaken in the name of accuracy and authenticity, as will be demonstrated in the following chapters, films seldom reproduce exact replicas of, say, historical or even contemporary fashions. As Pam Cook has pointed out, an element of contemporaneity is always present 'in a constant activity of *bricolage**' (1996: 45). The process of adaptation thus relates to the complex time-frame which is involved in any representation: the period in which the film is set and the period when it was released being the most obvious convergence. Different versions of the same or similar narratives are an interesting way to analyse this intertextual process, as demonstrated by case studies of versions of the Titanic disaster and two film adaptations of Patricia Highsmith's novel *The Talented Mr Ripley* (1955). One of the key issues relating to James Cameron's *Titanic* is the extent to which the costumes are 'made suitable' for both the narrative and the implied audience. As what I shall refer to as an adaptive text, a film such as *Titanic* makes many intertextual borrowings, seeking to place itself as a work of representation in relation to the historical account and memory of a terrifying event, and also in relation to previous representations such as *A Night To Remember* (Roy Baker, 1958). In this process, costume plays an integral role as an aspect of mise-en-scène.

The films chosen as case studies provide examples of how to analyse the role of costume in relation to a discussion of the following themes: realism; adaptation; narrative and characterization; spectacle; and identity/sexuality/gender. The films have been selected as examples that particularly invite the intertextual approach outlined above. The issues they raise can be applied to other films, genres and national cinemas; their function here is to serve as comparative rather than as exemplary texts. Chapter One foregrounds the issues of realism and authenticity, as well as demonstrating how costume can be used to delineate class and sexuality. Although James Cameron strove to represent 'the truth' and historical accuracy in *Titanic*, the costuming was highly influenced by generic concerns, as well as a preoccupation with contemporary notions of 'heritage'. Chapter Two explores aspects of male identity and sexuality by comparing two film versions of Patricia Highsmith's novel *The Talented Mr Ripley*. The main emphasis is on Minghella's film, starring Matt Damon and Jude Law. The differences between the two characters they play (Tom and Dickie), together with a theme of homosexual desire, serve as explorations of different facets of masculinity and sexual identity. The film's costumes assist in this task with, as I shall argue, significant results. They are used to facilitate the desire of one character to 'lose himself' in another's identity, thus highlighting the inherent instability of masculine identity as well as the unintended consequences of disguise. Chapter Three continues to explore the theme of identity, but this time from a female perspective in an analysis of *Desperately Seeking Susan*. In this film, Madonna's star persona works as a significant intertextual factor in both the narrative and the costuming.

In contrast to films which use costume as an adjunct to spectacle, for example *Titanic* or *The Matrix*, Chapter Four considers how costume is used in realist films such as *Wonderland* which claim to represent 'the ordinary' – to convey what is considered to be an accurate representation of 'everyday' dress in the realist terms of the characters presented. Such an approach will consider the extent to which films attempt to convey something of how, as Joanne Entwistle puts it: 'Fashion, dress and consumption provide ways of dealing with the problems of the modern world, characterized by increasing fragmentation and a sense of chaos. Fashion opens up possibilities for framing the self, however temporarily' (Entwistle 2000: 139). Although the costuming is less obtrusive than in the other films considered in this book, *Wonderland* nevertheless displays a careful attention to sartorial detail in its delineation of characters. Their clothes do not distract from the main trust of the narrative but serve as an integral element of establishing verisimilitude. I shall argue that their function can also be related to the film's overall representation of the modern city as a site of vulnerable, fragmented and shifting identities. In their different ways *Wonderland* and *The Matrix*, the focus of Chapter Five, therefore deal with questions of postmodern identity and society. *The Matrix* shows how, from the perspective of *retro film noir** and science fiction, a critique of postmodern society can be problematised by the film's use of costume, providing an example of how the 'language' of clothes operates in an excessive manner, demonstrating the complex pleasures of sartorial display as well as relating to discourses about costume and the body.

Above all, studying films 'through the clothes' enhances an appreciation of cinema which is primarily visual. It also draws attention to complex and often contradictory narrative structures; questions of stardom (as Madonna's use of screen fashions attests in the analysis of *Desperately Seeking Susan*); and to representations of gender on screen. The case studies that follow therefore demonstrate different facets of the analysis of screen costumes in popular mainstream films, with the exception of *Wonderland* which could also be defined as an art-house British film. Questions of national identity are pertinent to the study of fashion and even in big-budget films like *Titanic,* Hollywood seeks to cross national boundaries by using fashions for historical accuracy but also to appeal to contemporary tastes in international markets, in this case 'heritage' wear. Similarly, while *Desperately Seeking Susan* is an American film, the fashions can be related to both American and British punk. Set in Italy, *The Talented Mr Ripley* re-creates American fascination with European tastes and fashions while at the same time addressing issues of masculinity and sexual identity. In this way the work of costume designers emerges as a crucial contribution to film art, not just the 'big names' which have been chronicled in coffee-table accounts of celebrated couturiers who designed for the screen such as Hubert de Givenchy, Cecil Beaton or Christian Dior but also the teams of designers whose work has been distinctive and influential (see Chierichetti 1976). Costumes therefore have the potential to extend a film's national origin by facilitating the pursuit of an international audience while at the same time relating to its own national identity and culture. This simultaneous outward and inward address expands a film's sense of place and space. Similarly, as most film costumes illustrate, they can extend a film's sense of time since they relate both to the period in which the film is set but also to when it was produced and released. Edith Head described the costume designer's work as 'a cross between magic and camouflage' (1978: 36), to consolidate or alter an actor's image from film to film. Demystifying film fashion shows that it reaches much, much further.

1   TITANIC: DRESSING FOR DISASTER

> I wanted to be able to say to an audience, without the slightest
> pang of guilt: This is real. This is what happened. Exactly like this.
> (James Cameron, quoted in Marsh 1998: vi).

The quest for realism was made very clear from the planning stages of
Titanic, James Cameron's 1997 film version of the nautical disaster. As
with most films which are based on an historical event, it was considered
to be extremely important to get the details correct, so that audiences
would be convinced that 'This is real'. Cameron's choice of words is
telling: he would have felt guilty if he had not attempted to re-create
the past in an accurate manner, anything less would be sacrilegious, an
insult to the memory of those who died on the new White Star liner which
sank on its first voyage to New York in 1912 after colliding with an iceberg
off Newfoundland. This chapter will analyse the extent to which realist
aspirations in two (there were more, but this study will concentrate on
two) different film versions of the Titanic disaster limit the function of
costume as an 'excessive' system. Although based on the same events, *A
Night To Remember* (Roy Baker, 1958) and *Titanic* differ in their treatment
of costume, the former film restricting it to a functional, differential
role while the latter, certainly for the first hour of the film, utilizes it

in a far more emblematic manner as a means of exploring themes such as class identity, sexual awakening, 'Europeanness', bohemianism and heritage.

A Night To Remember, based on Walter Lord's 1956 best-selling novel, is faithful to the British tradition of 'quality realism', that is, cinema which aims to deliver a well-crafted, 'authentic' product with 'good' acting and demonstrating a high educative value. As John Hill has pointed out, the conception of what constitutes a 'good film' is often based around twin expectations concerning both narrative (cohesion; elements of repetition and difference and 'belief' in the characters) and 'realism' (conventions of what constitutes 'the real' which change over time) (1986: 53-4). While this might seem an appropriate aspiration for most entertainment films, in the late 1950s British context it acquires a particular significance. Expectations of realism depended on filmic conventions and liberal/humanist ideological assumptions which can be discerned in British films of the period. In many ways, A Night To Remember looks back to earlier films which shared its concern to depict, for example, class relations as uncomplicated and questions of sexuality and emotion as 'under wraps'. As a film that basically supports the status quo, A Night To Remember emphasises the heroism of the ship's officer class, particularly through the selfless efforts of Second Officer Lightoller (Kenneth More), and, with a few exceptions, in general the upper-class passengers are depicted as civil, 'natural' leaders. The most obvious elements of class critique in A Night To Remember are levelled against the ordinary seamen and the steerage passengers who are on several occasions the object of ridicule. With hindsight, therefore, the film says as much about 1958 as it does about 1912: the context of 1912 is being used to articulate concerns about British society just before the onset of considerable social and political change in the 1960s.

The primary narrative device used in A Night To Remember is to juxtapose the suspense of knowing how much time the ship has left before sinking – nearly two hours – with the failure of the Californian, the ship which is nearest to the Titanic, to pick up the wireless signals calling for assistance or to recognise the rockets fired on deck as signs of distress. Much of this narrative of 'human failing', beginning with Captain Smith of the Titanic's decision, against his better judgement, to accelerate the ship's speed in waters which have been reported as dangerous, is centered around problems of communication. In particular, the wireless operator's inability to send distress calls because the system is blocked with passengers' messages to family and friends which take on a trivial but tragic significance. This makes an interesting comparison with the German propaganda film *Titanic* (Herbert Selpin and Werner Klinger, 1943) which developed something of a class critique by depicting the wireless operator as being over-preoccupied with Bruce Ismay's business concerns, especially the White Star Line's shares whose value was related to the likelihood of the ship making a speed record for a transatlantic crossing.

Within this overarching suspense dynamic there is little opportunity for extended characterization, let alone a love story as in Cameron's version. As such, costume is not allowed to distract from the overall purpose of being faithful to the 'facts' which by 1958 had almost become myth: White Star Line managing director Bruce Ismay's escape; the tragedy of the deficiency of lifeboats and the cheery stoicism of the 'unsinkable' Molly Brown, not named in *A Night To Remember*, but unmistakably present.

There are some explicit references to and usages of costume, however, which provide some interesting contexts for *A Night To Remember* and may have inspired some of the emphases in Cameron's film. The film's depiction of different classes being faced by the same disaster nevertheless represents those classes as distinct and 'watertight'. Cross-class relations are forbidden and the suggestion of class mobility is unthinkable. The film opens with the launch of RMS Titanic by a woman

Figure 1: Stoic and dependable: Charles Lightoller (Kenneth More) in uniform and pullover in *A Night To Remember*.

dressed in a large-brimmed hat with men on either side of her wearing top hats which they remove when she makes her speech. The ship is thus aligned from the start with the upper-class whom we are to subsequently recognize very easily by their costume coding. The officers' uniforms resemble the attire worn by many of the upper-class male passengers, particularly that of the ship's designer, Thomas Andrews, whose suits are dark and austere. While the women's dress is elaborate, it is not excessive or depicted as frivolous. In this way the upper-classes wear their own sort of 'uniform' which is appropriate to their status. The film deals with *types* who can be easily recognized, a strategy which it uses throughout. The lower classes are all dressed in instantly recognisable drab clothing, usually with the men wearing flat caps and the women shrouded in shawls and long skirts.

Charles Lightoller is the moral centre of the film and the nearest we get to a sustained characterization. Throughout the disaster he is heroic, selfless and dependable. Although he wears uniform for most of the film he is identified, particularly during the ship's final hour, with his thick, large-collared woollen jumper. As an item of clothing it stands for his dependability and his stoicism, an article which provides comfort in the freezing conditions but also serves as an appropriate symbol of his importance as the man who gives orders and supervises much of the lifeboat operation with professionalism and sensitivity. This fits in with Kenneth More's image in the 1950s as a hero, the epitome of British male stoicism. A top box-office star, he often appeared as an officer-professional and is perhaps best known for his performance as Douglas Bader in *Reach for the Sky* (Lewis Gilbert, 1956). He carried his consistent 'persona' with him across a wide range of films, a persona that displayed 'a resolute, chivalrous integrity, a "rugged spiritual health", which is tested but never found wanting' (*Observer*, 11 October 1959, quoted by Spicer in Murphy 1997: 151). The contrasting, critical portrayal of Lightoller in Cameron's *Titanic* caused considerable controversy.

Instead of Kenneth More's easy, gentle but decisive characterization, Jonny Phillips' Lightoller is insensitive, unstable and nervous, and he is uniformed throughout. The impression is of someone who is rigid, a person who needs rules and regulations and without much personality. He hides behind his uniform and does not respond well to the crisis.

There are a few allusions to fashion in *A Night To Remember* which suggest some interesting nuances in an otherwise straightforward treatment of film costume. In a sequence near the beginning of the film before the ship has departed on its transatlantic crossing, Lightoller tells his wife that he will bring her scarlet Parisian silk garters back from New York, the implication being that the voyage will facilitate sexuality and exoticism on his return, a theme which Cameron develops in *Titanic*, as well as the European angle. As the ship 'shrinks' the world, commodities which cannot be purchased at home introduce new fashions and new ideas, suggesting mobility and challenges to tradition. This is an interesting instance of the use of costume as an implied means of introducing sexuality after travel, although in the case of Lightoller's wife, this is vicarious – her experience of travel and 'broadening of the mind' will occur because of the clothes her husband has chosen for her. As such they therefore stand in for experience, indicating that the potential for sexual awakening is already there, all it needs is for the clothes (and Lightoller) to give it permission to surface.

Although they would appear to be unremarkable, the use of lifejackets can be related to the theme of class. When 'Molly Brown' is persuading an upper-class woman to put on a lifejacket she coaxes her: 'Everyone's wearing them this season, they're the latest thing'. It is interesting that Benjamin Guggenheim is also reluctant to wear a lifejacket, as if to do so would rob the upper-class of its easily identifiable uniform, leading to a situation whereby class identity is lost as everyone has to don a lifejacket, the 'uniform' of disaster but also the uniform worn, on this occasion, by all classes. Guggenheim's remark, 'We have dressed in our best and are prepared to go down like gentlemen' is repeated in Cameron's *Titanic*. His appearance in full dress was based on eye-witness reports of the real event, represented in both films. In *A Night To Remember* he also asks those who are pressing the offensive lifejacket on him to tell his wife that in rejecting it he 'behaved decently'. In this way the film's stance on class is supported, not critiqued. Even wearing their lifejackets, many of the upper-class women continue to wear elaborate hats which differentiate them from the mass of terrified passengers, each struggling to find a place on a lifeboat. It is perhaps ironic that one of these hats plays an important plot role later on in the film when it is lit, held up and burned in order to attract the attention of the approaching Carpathia, the ship that rescued the survivors and carried them to New York.

In keeping with the conventions of realist films which were concerned to be instructive and socially useful in the Griersonian tradition, at the end of *A Night To Remember* the audience is reassured that disaster can be a learning experience, with rolling text which reminds us that after the tragedy no ship sailed without adequate lifeboat provision and the monitoring of icy conditions by 'the international ice patrol' alerted ships to the dangers of icebergs. David Lubin has stressed the importance of reading this film with contemporary politics in mind as 'a Cold War fable about the need for preparedness and competent military and class leadership' (1999: 78). Indeed, despite the film's realist aesthetic and form, the aspects of the disaster which it highlights constitute an address to contemporary, rather than historic concerns. A similar conclusion can be drawn about Cameron's *Titanic* which also has realist aspirations but contains an address to the 1990s which can be related to aspects of its costuming.

Titanic interweaves the ship's story with a fictional, cross-class romance between Jack Dawson, a poor working-class American with a talent for drawing who wins his ticket on the Titanic at a poker game just before the ship sails, and Rose Dewitt Bukater, a well-connected young woman who is returning to America with her mother to marry Cal Hockley, the son of a rich steel magnate who is also travelling on the Titanic. The inclusion of a love story has fundamental consequences for the costuming of *Titanic* since it facilitates a far more nuanced treatment of clothing than was required in *A Night To Remember*. Costumes are used to indicate social class but also to introduce the themes of modernity, sexuality and nationality. They are also used to celebrate a style which can be referred to as heritage, exploiting contemporary interest in fashions from the Victorian and Edwardian periods and showcasing current designs, particularly menswear, which have been inspired by elements of those styles.

The relationship between costume and class has been the subject of several key sociological studies, such as Thorstein Veblen's theory of 'conspicuous consumption', first published in 1899 in his book *The Theory of the Leisure Class*. Veblen argued that at the end of the nineteenth century clothes were used as indicators of social class and wealth. The monied bourgeoisie, 'the leisure class', in particular sought to emulate the aristocratic upper-classes by displaying their wealth via an elaborate and ever-changing wardrobe, with new fashions being determined by the constant need to demonstrate enhanced social status based on wealth. A man would dress his wife in the latest fashions – usually impractical clothes which made it clear that she did not work – thus serving as a sartorial expression of his increasing wealth and leisure. Although aspects of Veblen's theory have been critiqued from a more contemporary perspective – particularly by Wilson (1985: 50-3), Kunzle (1982), Steele (1985) and Entwistle (2000: 58-66), who dispute his conception of fashion as necessarily wasteful and oppressive, projected onto women in a negative way with them exercising no personal agency in choosing what to wear – elements of his analysis are pertinent to the deployment of costume in *Titanic*.

Cal's treatment of Rose, his fiancée, as a possession is most striking. In one of the dining-room scenes he is congratulated on her, as if she was a rare and valuable ornament. As the son of a steel magnate Cal is conscious of his status and of the need to 'train' Rose to behave in a way which he feels is appropriate to her future position as his wife. When he gives her 'The Heart of the Ocean', the diamond necklace which once belonged to Louis XVI, in a scene which implies that in exchange she must continue to grant him sexual favours after what we assume has been their first night together, he reminds her: 'We are royalty, Rose'. As a representative of industrial wealth, Cal imagines that his purchase of the diamond will raise his social status to aristocratic proportions. His gift to Rose, which she describes as 'overwhelming', is intended as a visual reminder of his wealth and, in Veblen's terms, an indicator of 'conspicuous consumption'. Rose's dilemma is whether to reject the destiny which has been selected for her, the destiny of marrying a man she does not love for the sake of saving her family from financial ruin. When her mother laces up her corset she reminds Rose that if she does not marry Cal she will have to suffer the indignity of having to work as a seamstress, the horror of being *déclassé**. While Rose and her mother have a 'good name', they need Cal's money in order to maintain it. The personal price Rose would have to pay for this is to surrender herself to Cal's vanity, to become another of his prized possessions which serve as visible signs of his enhanced social status. In this scene the corset therefore binds her to her fate, representing the repression of women in the Victorian and Edwardian periods. In the expectation that she will conform to her mother's wishes, Rose is being denied any freedom of choice. There is no sense here of the corset operating as an erotic object, as argued by David Kunzle (1982) in his work on Victorian women and tight-lacing.

In this way, dress and accessories are integral to the film's stance on class: both are used to signify and expose subtle divisions within

Figure 2: Ruth Dewitt Bukater (Frances Fisher) and Molly Brown (Kathy Bates) in contrasting attire in *Titanic*.

the upper-class. Although, for example, Molly Brown is accepted as one of the first-class passengers, Ruth Dewitt Bukater snubs her at every opportunity. Molly is often distinguished by outfits that are brasher than those worn by Ruth and the other upper-class women. When we first see her she is dressed in a red hat and furs and later, when she joins the other women at tea, her dark green dress contrasts with their cream dresses which are made of lighter, lacy fabrics and are coded as being more appropriate for the occasion of afternoon tea. As 'new money' (Ruth's description of her), Molly never gets it quite right and this is expressed by Ruth's reactions to her and also in the codes of her costumes: Molly may have money but she does not have aristocratic taste.

Deborah Scott designed the costumes for *Titanic* and was keen to depict changes in women's fashions from the Victorian period, represented by Ruth, Rose's mother, to a straighter, more modern, emancipated look for Rose. Since the ship was new and first-class tickets were expensive, many of the passengers were 'leisured' and fashion-conscious, having been to Paris before boarding the ship. In her quest for realism, Scott examined authentic photographs of passengers and researched the colours of contemporary fabrics as well as the shifts in styles which occurred in the first decade of the twentieth century (see Marsh 1998: 37-41). Costumes thus perform an *authenticating role*** as well as relating to the intertwined stories of the ship and Rose and Jack's romance. It is important to note, however, that many of the costumes are anachronistic. While film costume designers frequently claim inspiration from the past, the clothes will inevitably be influenced by generic traditions as well as by contemporary ideas. Costume is used to emphasize the film's critique of class, for example. Although they are from completely different class backgrounds, the film works towards Rose and Jack being increasingly similar, with Rose eventually living the kind of life that Jack might also have lived, as an adventurous person whose destiny relates to the modernity of the twentieth century rather than to the restrictions of the Victorian period. We know that after the disaster Rose changed her surname to Dawson, rejected her privileged background and at the end of the film we see a series of photographs which show us 'highlights' of her life as a mobile woman who rides horses (not side-saddle) and flies aeroplanes. In projecting its critique of rigid class structures, the film demonstrates many different usages of costume, some of which are stereotypical while others are more nuanced and subtle.

*Stereotypical costuming*** is used for the steerage passengers who represent a far more international grouping than in *A Night To Remember*. We have instantly recognisable representatives of many nationalities including Chinese, East European and Irish which is perhaps indicative of Cameron's desire to relate the film to the theme of immigration. The ship becomes 'the ship of dreams', representing faith in modernity and optimism about America, the 'new world'. It is significant that the only working-class characters who are not portrayed in a sympathetic light are English, in contrast to Welsh and Irish passengers whom we assume are emigrating to America. The ship's destiny towards the Statue of Liberty is emphasized when Fabrizio, Jack's Italian friend who also won his passage at the poker game, imagines that he can almost see the statue as they celebrate their luck by standing at the rail of the ship's prow as it races along, arms outstretched with the wind in their hair (an action Jack is later to perform with Rose).

The film's critique of class is, however, limited in the sense that its main representative, Jack, is differentiated very much from the other steerage passengers, in particular from Irishman Tommy Ryan who introduces himself to Jack on deck, just before Jack first sees Rose. Tommy is burly and dark-haired, dressed in labourer's clothes and wearing a bowler hat. His costume is stereotypical, resembling that worn by a model of a 'typical worker' in a costume museum. When Tommy sees Jack looking up at Rose he tells him that she is out of his reach, reminding him of his class background: 'Forget it, boyo. You're as likely to have angels fly out of your arse as to get next to the likes of her.' Ironically, the way Jack is dressed implies that acquaintance with her is, perhaps, not an impossible dream. Jack looks more delicate than Tommy, wearing a grey shirt with corduroy trousers held up by braces, providing a link with the present, with contemporary consumer culture. When Jack prevents Rose from jumping off the ship, he is wearing the costume of an 'outdoor boy' – a tartan-patterned jacket which resembles contemporary men's outdoor clothing, with its use of practical, but fashionable fabrics which are quite expensive. The fabrics are soft, greys and browns, providing a contrast with Cal's outfits which are generally made of harsher material in black and white. In combination with the star appeal of Leonardo DiCaprio, the contemporary, 'outdoor' costuming makes Jack even more appealing to contemporary audiences, an observation that qualifies Cameron's commitment to realism. In the scene when Jack tries

Figure 3: Artistic affinities: Rose (Kate Winslet) and Jack (Leonardo DiCaprio) on deck in *Titanic*.

to see Rose when she is in the chapel he wears a collarless shirt and a grey jacket, again dressed in a way which distinguishes him from the rest of the steerage passengers and connecting him with a style of menswear fashionable in the 1990s. In this way he is coded as different, the film's real aristocrat who 'shines up like a new penny' when he wears the dinner-suit Molly Brown has bought for her son.

Jack's difference is also expressed by his affinity with the arts. Jack represents European *bohemianism** and his talent for drawing separates him from the rest of the working-class passengers on the ship. When Rose is walking with him on deck after he has saved her life, she rebukes him for his rudeness when he asks her whether she loves Cal. This is a key moment in the film when their friendship could have ended. Instead, Rose asks him what he is carrying and he proceeds to show her his drawings. From that moment he acquires the cultural capital of the artist and is thus more acceptable to her. She describes his talent as 'unique', possessing a 'gift' which is enhanced by his familiarity with Paris and his drawings which reveal an openness about sexuality and an artistic appreciation of the body. Just as Rose and Jack admire the work of Degas, Picasso and Monet, Cal despises their taste. Audiences laugh as Cal remarks that Picasso 'won't amount to a thing', equating Jack and Rose's superior taste with ours: they share their cultural capital with the audience and in so doing align themselves with us. The implication is that Rose has a vision for modern art, for painters like Picasso, unlike Cal who would probably have thought more of them if they had been as expensive as the Heart of the Ocean. This scene works better for the purposes of the film than for historical accuracy, however. As Lubin has pointed out, in 1912 Picasso was already a notable artist whose paintings were rising in value (1999: 34).

In every way, Jack functions as the antithesis of Cal whose class and character is also expressed through dress. Our first view of Cal is on the quayside, just as his party is about to board the Titanic. In this scene his clothes are not particularly distinctive: he is wearing a grey suit which does not distract from the far more impressive introduction of Rose. But once he is on board we see that he is fashionable, wearing a beautifully tailored white waistcoat. He wears contrasting black and whites and his hair is glossed and slicked-down in a very precise way, unlike Jack's which is freer and more dishevelled. Although Cal is dressed fashionably, the fastidiousness of his attire is expressive of his controlling personality and his fixation with the idea that he is a 'gentleman', 'royalty'. Like Ruth, Cal knows how to dress for the ship's various meals, aware of the key sartorial distinctions between lunch and dinner. At lunch, when the building and naming of the ship, are being discussed, it is noticeable that Thomas Andrews, *Titanic*'s designer, is wearing a formal wing-collar (the same costume he wears throughout the film) whereas Cal and Bruce Ismay, who is also coded as fashionable, wear more modern, fold-down collars and ties. This is illustrative of their interest in novelty, particularly the speed of the ship whereas Andrews, an engineer/professional, represents traditional values which are associated with craftsmanship, solidity and practicality. He tells Rose that his original designs for the ship made ample provision for more lifeboats but he was forced to revise them because the White Star Line and, by implication Bruce Ismay, wanted more deck room, placing style over practicality. This simple difference between the shirts worn by Andrews and Cal and Ismay therefore relates to their different class identities and personalities, illustrating the key contribution made by costume in a film which constructs its mise-en-scène with such care and precision. As businessmen, the practical and unfussy shirts also represent their status as ambitious entrepreneurs (see Craik 1994: 188).

Rose's costumes are particularly interesting and as a major character she is introduced as a young woman in a striking way. We first see her from a high angle, above the car, a gloved-hand being taken by the chauffeur. She is wearing a black and white suit, with black lapels and collar and tie, which codes her as a young, modern woman. Her face is hidden by a large-brimmed, purple hat with a huge striped bow, until she looks up at the gigantic ship. The choice of purple is significant in view of the film's development of Rose as an emancipated 'new woman', purple and white (green also, but not used here) being associated with the *suffragette movement**. The 'new woman' of the early twentieth century was associated with the quest for greater female independence and the campaigns in both Britain and the United States for votes for women (see Rowbotham 1997: 36-39). Consequently, Rose's clothes are in stark contrast to those worn by her mother who is dressed in a formal green coat with a blouse buttoned up to the neck, and has a dark hat with a feather on top.

Once on board ship, Rose's costumes relate strongly to her character, particularly her affinity with Jack as a 'free spirit', lover of the arts and to her emerging sexuality. Although her clothes are the finest, there are hints of her rebellion from an early stage. When she is at lunch with her mother, Cal, Molly Brown, Thomas Andrews and Bruce Ismay, her hair is slightly looser than the other women's; she smokes a cigarette which Cal snatches from her when her mother complains and her dress is loose and green. When she gets up from the table we see that there is a red sash around her middle with a rose fastened in the front. The colour red is frequently worn by Rose: when she is threatening to jump off the ship her dress is coloured red at the bottom and she is wearing red shoes. This bears an intertextual relationship with Vicky (Moira Shearer) in *The Red Shoes* (Powell and Pressburger, 1948), as the dancer who commits suicide wearing red ballet shoes.

This film also uses the colour red to signify sexuality, in keeping with the Hans Christian Anderson fairytale about the red ballet shoes which force their wearer to dance on and on, indicating a fatal attraction towards movement and, by implication, sexuality. The use of the colour red here is, of course, anachronistic, serving to underscore the film's theme of Rose's sexual awakening. Once Rose has made up her mind to stay with Jack, and after he has drawn her, she puts on a loose, pastel-coloured dress with many layers of *diaphanous material**. Whilst this is symbolic of her freedom and sexual satisfaction with Jack, it is also useful for the plot because her costume does not restrict her when making the agile movements she is required to perform for the rest of the film when the ship is sinking.

As well as these indications of class and sexuality, costume is used as a key element of plot in *Titanic* on several occasions. In his quest to repress Rose's rebelliousness, Cal is assisted by his manservant, Lovejoy, who takes on Cal's intense dislike of Jack. This is first signalled by Lovejoy noticing that Jack removed his boots and coat when he was supposed to have rescued Rose when she slipped off the rail, nearly falling to her death, remarking that he would not have had time to remove the items if the incident happened as they described: he suspects that they have lied. Jack steals a coat and hat so that he can find Rose on the first-class deck. The coat is later used against him when Lovejoy plants the diamond in its pocket to prove that Jack is a thief and he is further damned when the coat is revealed to be stolen. On this evidence he is handcuffed to a pipe, unable to escape when water floods into the crew passage, facilitating one of the most suspenseful sequences in the film when Rose rescues him by splitting the handcuff chain with an axe. Later, Cal loses the diamond by putting a coat on Rose without remembering that it is in the pocket: miraculously, it stays there with Rose, surviving the ordeal and in so doing linking an item of clothing with an accessory which is vital for the plot of the film.

Costume is also used at another key narrative moment when Rose makes her decision to tell Jack that she will leave Cal and her mother for him. We see her sitting in the first-class dining room, looking at a little girl on another table who is being trained, just as she was, to be a 'lady'. The child is dressed impeccably in a cream dress with lace tiers and is being taught to sit up straight and place her napkin carefully on her lap when eating. She looks like a smaller image of her mother who is sitting opposite her, and they both wear elaborate hats: both conform to the expected social norms.

As well as signalling a key change in plot, this small incident is symbolic of Rose's rejection of her upbringing and of the life that has been mapped out for her by her mother. As in *A Night To Remember*, but in a different context, a hat is used at a crucial moment. When Cal is searching for Rose on board the Carpathia she is wearing a shawl over her head but could still quite easily be recognised. As Cal passes her he looks in her direction but at that moment a woman passes between them wearing a hat which obscures his view: we are spared an embarrassing reunion by the intervention of a hat! The film uses an accessory – the diamond necklace, the Heart of the Ocean – as a key plot element as well as in a symbolic way, as analysed by Adrienne Munich and Maura Spiegel (1999: 155-68). They interpret the diamond as a 'unifying object' in *Titanic* which:

> changes in meaning as the object itself passes through different levels of the film's plotting. It is first the primary object of Brock Lovett's treasure hunt, then the prized possession of industrialist Cal Hockley, and then a sentimental reminder of Rose Bukater's liberating love for Jack Dawson. Not only does the Heart of the Ocean carry the movie's ostensible message about proper and improper relations to wealth and property, and even to life itself, but it also embodies its thematic of secrets, memory, access to the past, and the female heart. Like the fetish it is, the diamond's commodity and symbolic value signifies even beyond the movie's plot, extending to lived reality, as the movie interacts with history, with movie history, with the media, and with the audience and its desires (155).

In this way the necklace exceeds the demands of plot, performing a function which can be described as 'excessive'. At first representing materialism and masculine possessiveness, the diamond's changing significance throughout underscores the film's critique of wealth and assertion of democratic values. Somewhat ironically, and coinciding with the film's release, replicas of the necklace were on sale as tie-in merchandise (157).

From these analyses of two versions of the Titanic disaster it is clear that as a key element of mise-en-scène, costume is capable of conveying many complex meanings. As we have seen, while a director might proclaim an overall commitment to realism, this is compromised by the tension between authenticating processes and narrative pleasure. 'Authenticating processes' refer to the ways in which films based on historical fact are obligated to present some semblance to 'the truth' as it has come to be understood. This of course depends on the extent of public knowledge about that particular event and in the case of the Titanic, both Baker and Cameron could assume that most people knew something about the details of the disaster. They would also have certain expectations about what people wore in 1912. As we have seen, however, the quest for authenticity was compromised by the imperatives of the melodramatic narrative. This was not necessarily inconsistent with audiences' *perception* of the period, as generic verisimilitude dominated the 'preferred' reading. As the opening quotation to this chapter demonstrates, Cameron was motivated by an intense desire to present 'the truth', using computer technology and an almost life-size model of the ship to present an account which was able to show the ship and its sinking in a far more extensive and spectacular way than was possible in 1958. As the box-office attests, people were persuaded that his version gave them something which they thought 'rang true'.

Since *A Night To Remember* concentrated on the suspense narrative of communication problems, its costumes were used for authenticating purposes in a fairly shorthand manner with, as I have shown, some interesting exceptions. As we have already noted, the casting of Kenneth More as Second Officer Lightoller is particularly significant and can be linked to More's star persona in the 1950s. Lightoller is given a major role in Baker's version but there is nothing that detracts from his primary function as representing the heroism and stoicism of the professional/officer class: his trusty pullover confirms this idea. *Titanic*, on the other hand, included a melodramatic love story, thus introducing generic elements which dictated a different role for costume. This required more extensive usages which relate to the film's need to satisfy expectations of narrative pleasure which are associated with melodrama and romance.

Leonardo DiCaprio's star persona and popularity with teenage fans meant that he had to be dressed in order to enhance his current appeal, and his fashionable 'leisure' clothing present him as a not particularly convincing fictional character from 1912 but, more importantly, as one of the most popular male stars of 1997. Codes of verisimilitude therefore depend on their generic context and the 'authenticating process' in this instance was determined more by DiCaprio's image than by a desire to convince audiences that the 'correct' costumes had been used. This identity had been established with his casting as Romeo in *Romeo + Juliet* (Baz Luhrmann, 1996), an updated version which was set in present-day Verona Beach, complete with gang warfare, soundtrack CD and dazzling imagery. Another story of forbidden love, *Romeo + Juliet* was an excellent precursor for DiCaprio, establishing his fan base so that by the time *Titanic* was released, his following, particularly among teenage girls, was ready to expand. Even though DiCaprio was reported as being uncomfortable with his status as a teen idol, the film gave rise to 'a group feeling of belonging' for his fans which found expression in discussions on the World Wide Web, the purchase of *Titanic* merchandise and of the large number of magazines which published DiCaprio interviews, features and pictures (see Nash and Lahti 1999: 64-88). The stylish irreverence of *Romeo + Juliet* also prepared the way for Cameron's presentation of DiCaprio as Jack, a character who could, to some extent, stand outside time, certainly outside 1912, with his articulation of 'American Dream' values and the promotion of democratic ideals which many viewers would like to think exist in contemporary society.

Film costumes therefore occupy a shifting place within film narratives. They can advance plot, suggest character and provide an authenticating discourse for films which are set in the past. In many ways they can 'exceed' the demands of the narrative by suggesting intertextual connections and allude to star identities which have been forged outside the narrative system of that particular film. As I have suggested, *Titanic* draws on audience expectations and produces pleasures which exceed the 'bare facts' of the disaster. The careful way in which costume is used to delineate social status reinforces a critique of class while at the same time privileges values which in their own way are exclusive. Jack and Rose are therefore a 'special couple' who are united by their good taste, love of adventure and insight into the hypocrisy of the upper-class. As such, Rose's costumes provide an indication of her rebellion; they are different from the other women's and provide pleasure in their suggestion of independence and sexuality. Her first costume is fascinating in that it is 'excessive' to the position of her character at that particular moment in the film. Our first view of Rose wearing her modern suit and enormous purple hat anticipates what she will become rather than what she is when she boards the Titanic. Just after we are introduced to her, the voice-over tells us of her predicament, of her status as a trapped woman, but her costume perhaps indicates otherwise. In her restricted lifestyle on board ship, subtle details of her costume – for example, the anachronistic red shoes – are used to suggest her emerging independence and sexuality. In this way, costume is used in a symbolic manner which exceeds the demands of authenticity. By contrasting what she wears and how she wears it with the rigid and formal outfits worn by her mother we are invited to develop a comparative appreciation of the work of film costume. As such, the sartorial elements of heritage presented in *Titanic* acquire a critical function, commenting on the vanities of the aristocracy, the minute distinctions developed by them in their protection of their lineage, as with Ruth's rejection of Molly Brown as 'new money', the irony being that without Cal's industrial millions Ruth and Rose will lose their social standing.

As the ship sinks, wealth and finery are destroyed. As in *A Night To Remember*, lifejackets become the essential garments as we see clothes, accessories, furniture and objects which have hitherto been presented as desirable and beautiful, destroyed, unable to offer protection or comfort in the face of disaster. One striking example of how costume is used as symbolic counterpoint is when we see rats running down the third-class corridor and then cut to a shot of Bruce Ismay's gold and black velvet slippers as he too runs from the water which is seeping into every orifice of the ship. We later see him, rat-like, skulking in a lifeboat as women and children drown.

The potential for film costume to break free from the strict demands of realism therefore depends in large part on genre, and romantic melodrama is certainly a genre which encourages such departures. The fashion system itself is contradictory and ambiguous and *Titanic* relates to both its function as indicator of social status but also to its expression of individual agency. Cameron's wish to persuade audiences that 'this is real' is therefore more complex than the reproduction of events, technology, costumes, accessories and furniture which equate with historical accounts, design manuals and catalogues.

2   THE TALENTED MR RIPLEY: COSTUMING IDENTITY

Tom was in a good humour. It was Paris. *Wonderful* to sit in a famous café, and to think of tomorrow and tomorrow and tomorrow being Dickie Greenleaf! The cuff links, the white silk shirts, even the old clothes – the worn brown belt with the brass buckle, the old brown grain-leather shoes, the kind advertised in *Punch* as lasting a lifetime, the old mustard-coloured coat sweater with sagging pockets, they were all his and he loved them all. And the black fountain pen with little gold initials. And the wallet, a well-worn alligator wallet from Gucci's. And there was plenty of money to go in it.

Patricia Highsmith's novel, *The Talented Mr Ripley*, first published in the USA in 1955, has inspired two film adaptations, *Plein Soleil* (René Clément, 1960) and *The Talented Mr Ripley* (Anthony Minghella, 1999). The story is about the desire of one man, Tom Ripley, to become another, Dickie Greenleaf, to change his *identity**, his social class and his appearance. One of the major ways this is achieved is through costuming: all three texts use clothes as a focus of plot, character and identity. In the latest adaptation in particular, costume is a key element for suggesting the mutability of identity but also of exploring an individual's pursuit to fix identity through appearance.

As Elizabeth Wilson has commented, fashion can be seen as 'one means whereby an always fragmentary self is glued together into the semblance of a unified identity' (1985: 12). But, as Joanne Entwistle notes, this 'semblance' creates a complex relationship to identity: 'on the one hand the clothes we choose to wear can be expressive of identity, telling others something about our gender, class status and so on; on the other, our clothes cannot always be "read", since they do not straightforwardly "speak" and can therefore be open to misinterpretation' (2000: 112). As we shall see, Ripley's desire to be a 'fake somebody' depends on the plausibility of his new persona. The clothes and other accoutrements of wealth give him the confidence to pull it off, momentarily secure in his new identity but at the same time entering a world of deception, danger and death.

In Highsmith's novel Tom Ripley, a young man down on his luck in New York, is recruited by Herbert Greenleaf, a wealthy shipping magnate, to go to Italy to persuade his errant playboy son, Dickie, an acquaintance of Tom, to return to the USA. Tom agrees, the trip providing an escape from financial worries and the promise of adventure. When Tom meets Dickie he is charmed by him and becomes fascinated with his way of life. They become friends and use some of the money given to Tom by Dickie's father to supplement an already lavish lifestyle and Tom moves into Dickie's house. Tom plans a future with Dickie, excluding his girlfriend, Marge, whom Tom dislikes and sees as a barrier between the two men's friendship.

The novel implies that Tom is a repressed homosexual and tension develops as Tom begins to realize that he is being dropped in favour of Marge. When Tom begins to have disagreements with Dickie he fantasizes about killing him and assuming his identity. With a talent for impersonation, Tom feels that he could get away with it, which he does after he has murdered Dickie on a boat in San Remo. The rest of the story is about Tom's masquerade, of his interchangeable identities as Dickie and Tom, his murder of Freddie Miles (Philip Seymour Hoffman), a friend of Dickie's who discovers the truth, and of his eventual escape, having fooled Dickie's father into believing that his son killed Freddie Miles and then committed suicide. The novel ends with an ironic twist as Herbert Greenleaf makes over Dickie's trust fund and properties to Tom, whom he sees as a loyal friend and responsible envoy, the son he never had.

This analysis will focus primarily on Minghella's version of the story, although *Plein Soleil* and the novel will be referenced on several occasions since they are key intertexts for the 1999 film. Many of the film's scenes are taken directly from the novel, with crucial differences in emphasis which affect our understanding of character. While Minghella's film, for example, makes the affluent, sun-kissed world of Dickie and Marge attractive, the novel and *Plein Soleil* expose its hypocrisies, distinctions and exclusions in a more sustained manner since their presentation of Dickie is more critical and less charismatic. Even so, as Chris Straayer has pointed out in her comparison of the novel and *Plein Soleil*, the novel allows Tom to adopt Dickie's identity more successfully than in *Plein Soleil*, the latter text refusing him to 'pass' acceptably or therefore transcend his lower class status (2001: 122).

In the novel, Dickie is a terrible painter who is neither profound nor highly intelligent; in *Plein Soleil* (Dickie is called Philippe in this version) he is snobbish and not so attractive or compelling as Tom who is played by French actor Alain Delon in his first major role. In Minghella's film, Dickie (Jude Law) is extremely handsome, a jazz enthusiast and saxophone player with considerable charm and wit. Similarly, there are key differences in the presentation of Marge, Dickie's girlfriend. While in the novel she is not 'bad-looking', a 'good egg' with not much intelligence and in *Plein Soleil* she is a rather bland love-object, first for Dickie and then for Tom, in *The Talented Mr Ripley* she grows in stature throughout the film, and becomes more mature. At the end she is the only character who realizes the truth about Tom but is not believed. As Charlotte O'Sullivan put it in her review of the film for *Sight and Sound*: 'Dickie and Marge are extraordinary, objects of sexual and economic desire perfectly formed to suit middlebrow audiences' (2000: 54). Costuming is a key indicator of these differences and central to all three texts' engagement with the theme of identity. The three texts also allow different articulations of homosexuality. As Straayer observes, the novel is more fluid about questions of class and sexual identity than *Plein Soleil* (2001: 128). As the following analysis will demonstrate, Minghella's version draws more on the novel's discourse about repressed homosexuality.

Tom's desire to escape from being a 'nobody' is presented as an understandable goal in Minghella's film. It all begins with a seemingly innocent mistake when Tom is spotted by Herbert Greenleaf because he is wearing a Princeton jacket, thinking that Tom must have been to Princeton and known Dickie in the 'class of fifty-six'. In fact, Tom borrowed the jacket to play the piano at a New York society wedding, standing-in for a friend who could not play because he injured his wrist. Tom does not reveal the truth when Mr Greenleaf invites him to visit his shipyards and asks him to go to Italy to reason with Dickie. This is different from the novel in which Tom knew Dickie and the device of the Princeton jacket is Minghella's addition.

It is ironic that after this incident we see Tom dressed in the uniform of a valet-boy at a concert hall, treated as a servant by the well-to-do men whose jackets he brushes: in this uniform he is invisible whereas with the Princeton jacket he is noticed, recognised as a member of the upper-class. As Tom prepares for his trip to Italy by learning about jazz so that he has something in common with Dickie, a jazz enthusiast, we see him in his dark, basement apartment wearing a crumpled white t-shirt, his scruffiest outfit, representative of his old life. By contrast, when he leaves for Italy he is dressed in a smart dark suit, as if he is starting a new life. In this way the film sets up a causal motivation for Tom: his pretence to Herbert Greenleaf seems to be harmless, a means of escape from a drab life. Minghella is therefore establishing an important role for clothes from the very start of his film, not only in terms of plot but also in relation to what they symbolise.

This emphasis is less marked in *Plein Soleil*. We are not shown the backstory. The film opens with Philippe (Dickie) and Tom already in Italy and we learn that Tom has known and 'worshipped him' since he was fifteen. Although the emphasis on costume is less marked than in *The Talented Mr Ripley*, our first sight of Tom and Philippe distinguishes them by their clothes in a significant but understated way. Tom is dressed conventionally, in a light blue shirt with the collar unbuttoned. The shirt is tucked into his trousers whereas Philippe is more casual, wearing a loose, unbuttoned, soft-textured, brown suede jacket which reveals his bare chest. Clearly an expensive quality item, despite his dishevelled appearance he is coded as fashionable and wealthy. Both are wearing pale trousers but Philippe's are rolled up to the calf, again conveying a more relaxed, fashionable and casual impression than that of Tom. Perhaps influenced by the costuming of *Plein Soleil*, Dickie wears calf-length trousers on several occasions in *The Talented Mr Ripley*.

Minghella's film continues to emphasise the importance of costume. The scene in *The Talented Mr Ripley* when Tom first sees Dickie and introduces himself is extremely significant and indicative of the pre-murder costuming which contrasts Tom's appearance with that of Dickie. Tom has arrived in Mongibello, the beautiful Italian resort where Dickie lives (a fictional place invented by Highsmith), first seeing Dickie and Marge through binoculars as they dive off a boat, a glamourous, sun-tanned couple. When Tom goes on the beach to introduce himself he is wearing brown leather shoes and tight, yellow-lime greenish woollen bathing trunks which look uncomfortable. He removes his shoes and he walks awkwardly on the sand. His skin is very pale and he looks completely out of place amongst the elegant, tanned Italians. Fitting closely, the trunks are also revealing, making Tom feel uneasy about appearing as a sexualised object in public. By contrast, Dickie's patterned cotton trunks are loose; he looks completely at ease on his sun-lounger next to Marge when Tom walks up and pretends that they met at Princeton. Tom's resourcefulness is, however, indicated in this scene because he turns the spectacle of his incongruity to his advantage. When Dickie comments on his white skin, Tom replies that it is 'undercoat', 'primer', which appeals to Dickie's sense of humour and leads to Marge's vague invitation of another meeting. It also points to Tom's gradual assumption of power within Dickie's milieu, his stark, pale body gradually evolving into a tanned and muscled spectacle. Actor Matt Damon's muscled body is, of course, anachronistic for the 1950s. It relates to Damon's star persona in the 1990s and serves to indicate Tom's increasing power in the narrative. It is a body that adapts to Dickie's lifestyle extremely well and indeed convinces that the body fits the clothes. When Tom later wears Dickie's clothes he can 'pass' convincingly as Dickie, illustrating how, as Jeffords (1989) and Segal (1990) argue, clothes can perform the function of masquerade, concealing masculine vulnerability as an assertive facade.

Before Tom murders Dickie, his clothes are indicative of his lower-class status; plain shirts and a jacket which contrast with Dickie's fashionable and expensive outfits discussed below. In Minghella's film, the jacket continues to be significant as an item of clothing as Tom's corduroy jacket appears many times and is commented on by Freddie Miles and Dickie, implying that he should exchange it for something more fashionable, in keeping with their chic attire. When Tom and Dickie go to Rome, Dickie promises that they will choose a new jacket for Tom who is disappointed when Freddie Miles appears and commandeers Dickie's time. They exclude Tom from a visit to a jazz club, leaving him to sight-see and with no time to purchase the jacket with Dickie. When Tom comments on this, Dickie says that he will give him one of his and this is followed by one of the most striking sequences in Mongibello when, thinking that Dickie is still in Rome, Tom dresses up in Dickie's clothes. The differences between this incident as presented in the three versions of the text illustrate their different emphases and usages of costume.

In the novel and in *Plein Soleil* the dressing-up scene is motivated by Tom's need to escape from the sight of Dickie and Marge together. In the novel he sees them kissing in Marge's house and runs back to Dickie's house in disgust, goes up to Dickie's room and puts on the trousers of a grey flannel suit, a blue and white striped shirt, a dark blue silk tie and a pair Dickie's shoes. Tom parts his hair on the other side and starts to imitate Dickie, telling Marge that he does not love her and simulates her strangulation: "I had to do that," he said, still breathlessly, addressing Marge, though he watched himself in the mirror. "You were interfering between Tom and me – No, not that! But there *is* a bond between us!" He then puts on a hat, as Highsmith describes: 'It was a little grey Tyrolian hat with a green-and-white feather in the brim. He put it on rakishly. It surprised him how much he looked like Dickie'.

Straayer has argued that this passage represents a significant development in that in recognizing his likeness in the mirror to Dickie he 'has produced Greenleaf and himself as a *couple*' (2001: 122). Dickie interrupts Tom's masquerade in an embarrassing moment, however, with Tom blurting out: 'Oh – just amusing myself'. Immediately after this incident Dickie tells Tom that Marge suspects him of being 'queer', a charge which he denies vehemently. The framing of the dressing-up scene within the context of Dickie's relationship with Marge and Tom's detestation of it is therefore important in linking the desire to be Dickie with the murder of Marge. At that point in the novel the obstacle appears to be Marge, not Dickie's indifference to and growing boredom with Tom. Tom is clearly unable to accept his homosexual desire for Dickie. He therefore imagines a violent scenario to prevent a repetition of the intense feelings of disgust he experienced when witnessing Dickie's love-making with Marge. This of course prefigures his later murder of Dickie, the real object of his desire.

In *Plein Soleil* the incident is also occasioned by Philippe (Dickie) and Marge's lovemaking, but this time they are all in the same apartment when Philippe and Tom have returned from Rome. Tom obviously feels left out, but there is not quite the same implication of disgust, he simply feels in the way. In this film, the homosexual context is not developed and Marge is not depicted as particularly repulsive to Tom (in fact he ends up having a sexual relationship with her). Bored, Tom goes into Philippe's room, kicks off his shoes and puts on Philippe's white loafers. The music is suspenseful, as we see him putting them on languorously, lying on the floor with his face obscured by open cases. Tom sits up and puts on a dark striped jacket, selects a tie and looks in the mirror. He brushes his hair, as in the novel, and the camera is behind Tom so we see his mirror-image. Kneeling on the floor, he leans forward and imitates a love-scene with Marge, mimicking Philippe's voice, 'Marge, my love, my sweet', wagging his finger, saying, 'my little Marge knows I love her and will never go away with the nasty man my father sent'. He then kisses the mirror and says 'Blinded by love of Marge'; he kisses the mirror again and is interrupted by Philippe. As Tom rises to his feet we see both men in the mirror, looking very similar. Tom quickly tussles his hair back and begins to take off the jacket; as in the novel, he says that he was amusing himself. Philippe looks surprised, there is no discussion of the masquerade, he simply tells him to take off his shoes.

While this is conveyed in a suspenseful manner, there is not quite the same sexual charge as in the novel. The use of mirrors is, however, creative, particularly the kisses which are symbolic in their implicit allusion to Tom's admiration for Philippe. They also have a homo-narcissistic function, as Straayer has observed, which might work to exclude Dickie rather than privilege him as an ego-ideal (2001: 120). Also, without the dialogue about Marge the scene would have a much more explicit insinuation of homosexual passion, as well as conveying the narcissistic bliss of the moment of Tom's recognition that he looks very much like Philippe. In general, therefore, the homosexual subtext is not as developed as it is in the novel.

To develop this interpretation, in a Lacanian reading this scene symbolises Tom's recognition of a more perfect image of himself as Philippe. When Tom dressses as Philippe he sees himself as a unified being, much as the child in the Lacanian 'mirror phase' sees itself in the mirror and experiences a moment of pure *jouissance** (jubilation), in contrast to the previous feeling of being uncoordinated and fragmented.

The moment of 'recognition' is, however, also a moment of 'misrecog-nition' in that the mother is also present, thus emphasizing the illusory status of the appearance of wholeness (see Hayward 2000: 286-306 for a summary of psychoanalytic concepts). In a similar scenario, but substituting Philippe for the (m)other, the appearance of the real Philippe shatters this illusion, leaving Tom with an even more fragmented sense of identity than before. From this perspective, Philippe's murder allows him to regain the enhanced sense of self he experienced when looking at himself in the mirror as Philippe rather than as Tom: in this reading the murder of Philippe is inevitable. It can also be linked to the Lacanian concept of 'The Real' which operates outside of the Imaginary and the Symbolic Orders and is associated with the 'unrepresentable' – death and desire. In Minghella's film, Tom hallucinates that he has seen Dickie after the murder, when he is riding down a narrow street on his Vespa scooter. Another image associated with the murder haunts Tom as he watches act two, scene two of Tchaikovsky's opera *Eugene Onegin*, which features a fatal duel between two male friends. These incidents are disturbing images for Tom as they are reminders of the repressed, not only of Dickie, but also homosexual desire: the death and desire which constitute 'The Real'.

In Minghella's *The Talented Mr Ripley* the dressing-up scene follows Tom's feelings of exclusion when Freddie and Dickie abandon him in Rome and Dickie does not buy him a new jacket as promised. As we see Tom board the train in Rome we hear a song which continues in the following scene (overlapping music between scenes is a technique often used by Minghella). Unlike *Plein Soleil*, in which the music is *non-diegetic** and used to create suspense, the music in *The Talented Mr Ripley* is *diegetic**, as Tom sings along to the lyrics of a record he has put on the gramophone. It is 'May I?' a popular romantic song performed by Bing Crosby with appropriate lyrics for someone who is in love with Dickie: 'May I, may I be the only one to say I, really fell in love the day I, first set eyes on you'. Tom is dressed in a dinner jacket with bow-tie, looking very smart until we see that he is not wearing trousers. This adds a brilliant, rakish detail to the costume, making it different, slightly ridiculous but in this context perfect for the effect of *camp**. He sings to the mirror, and dances elegantly towards a classical statue of the torso of a nude man, collecting a boater hat which is perched on the statue and then a silk scarf which he wraps over his shoulder in a grand gesture as he twirls around the floor. The whole routine is playful, executed with finesse and elegance. Just as Dickie comes into the room Tom is singing to the mirror, bottom stuck out, in a particularly campy manner, as Dickie says 'What on earth are you doing?', scratching the record as he angrily turns off the gramophone. Embarrassed by his state of half-undress, Tom goes behind the full-length mirror, his head visible above the top so that from Dickie's point of view we see an image which shows Dickie reflected in the mirror with Tom's head above, emphasising their similarity and prefiguring what is to come when Tom later adopts Dickie's persona. We have the same dialogue as in the other two versions, with Tom saying that he was amusing himself, but there is a far greater sense of disgust in Dickie's reaction. Tom implores him not to say anything to the others, but we later find out that he has told Freddie, thus rejecting Tom's invitation to share a secret.

This far more risqué sequence creates a very different impact from the other two versions. Its grace and wit enhances Tom's status as a performer, and the whole incident seems less about wanting to be Dickie in a sinister way and more about camping it up in homage to his growing attraction for him. The combination of the dinner jacket, no trousers and classical statue is a humorous but knowing allusion to his sexuality which implies a far more mature understanding of it than is evident in the rest of the narrative. It provides a brief moment of unguarded lightness after the introduction of Freddie in Rome, but afterwards the narrative continues with Tom's exclusion and gradual realization that Dickie does not have the same plans for the future or share similar feelings for him. The scratched record symbolises Dickie's refusal of Tom's romantic advances, a disavowal of the intimacy that Tom craves. From Dickie's point of view Tom's 'performance' represents a sinister invasion of his privacy. It is also a reminder of the latent homosexuality that threatens the 'normality' of his friendship with Tom.

Tom's clothes become much more distinctive after he has murdered Dickie. There is, however, some indication of things to come just before, when he accompanies Dickie to the San Remo jazz festival and Dickie tells him that he knows that they never met at Princeton. In San Remo Tom wears the same smart dark suit he wore as he was leaving New York, providing a neat sartorial sequencing to the doomed relationship with Dickie, occurring just before the dramatic scene on the boat when Dickie finally rejects Tom, calling him a 'leech', followed by the fight and Dickie's long drawn-out murder. The suit points to the darkness to come and to Tom's inability to deal with rejection, consigning him to a paradoxical life of insecurity after his violent outburst results in the death of his love-object. Once Dickie has been murdered and Tom pretends to be him he feels secure in his new identity but at the same time can never relax for fear of discovery: the 'wholeness' of his new identity is therefore illusory.

The first time we see Tom dressed as Dickie, he is checking into the Grand Hotel in Rome. Minghella intercuts this with him checking into another, down-at-heel hotel as Tom, to emphasize the difference between the confident rich young man who is welcomed and treated with respect and the rather shy, nondescript Tom who blends in with the harsh, darkish brown mise-en-scène of a cheap hotel. This technique allows us to appreciate the difference between what John Flügel refers to as 'confluence' and 'contrast'. According to Flügel 'confluence' involves costume which augments a person's physical appearance by extending the body's reach and impact, such as a smart, tailored suit and an expensive leather case; 'contrast', on the other hand, refers to clothes that do not quite fit, making the person appear insignificant, for example a baggy jacket or one which it too tight (see Rubinstein 1995: 7). As Dickie, Tom wears an elegant suit and begins to acquire an expensive wardrobe, assisted by Meredith (Cate Blanchett), a rich young American woman he met on arrival in Italy and who crops up on several occasions, the only person who thinks that he is Dickie from the very beginning. Tom's obsession with being Dickie is further emphasized when he has a new wallet embossed with Dickie's initials and wears Dickie's distinctive rings which he coveted earlier and wrested from his body after the murder. It is as if he needs to persuade himself of his new identity, providing himself with constant reminders which can be interpreted as an attempt to banish any feelings of insecurity. Sharp and smart for most of the film, Tom is careless in satisfying this craving for visible signs of his authenticity as Dickie, since therein lies the possibility of discovery. The clothes and accessories he favours are not simply those worn by someone of Dickie's class but items which can be clearly identified as belonging to Dickie Greenleaf. As such, they are therefore symbolic of Tom's quest for authenticity: they serve as a kind of hallmark, reminding him of his new persona and status. They can also be interpreted as Tom's desire to fetishise Dickie after his death, investing the rings in particular with sexual symbolism. They also function as a symbol of Tom's denial of his 'lack' – not being the real Dickie but at the same time desperately trying to keep him alive, as it were, in his own image.

As in the novel, the rings are also used as key elements of plot, creating tension as they serve as clues to Tom's guilt. When Freddie Miles visits Rome looking for Dickie, he tracks down the apartment registered in his name by Tom, and Tom has to struggle to remove the rings so that Freddie will not recognize them. Even so, Freddie becomes suspicious when he sees that Tom is wearing one of Dickie's embossed shirts and has slippers embroidered with his initials. The insinuation that Tom and Dickie are having a homosexual relationship is clear. Looking around the apartment, which is decorated according to Tom's taste, Freddie comments that 'the only thing that looks like Dickie is you'. In this instance the fact that Tom is wearing Dickie's clothes and jewellery does not give him protection. Instead it exposes his insecurity about his homosexuality as Freddie draws his own conclusions. Straayer points out that Dickie's upper-class masculinity is represented by his expensive clothes and affection for style but it is not, in this context, necessarily associated with homosexuality (2001: 126). But in this scene, and with Tom as the wearer, he is exposed as such in a way that intensifies his insecurity about having had homosexual feelings for Dickie: hence the necessity to murder the perceptive but threatening Freddie. As he is leaving, Freddie sees that the maid clearly thinks that Tom is Dickie and he returns to the apartment where Tom murders him. The rings continue to serve as an important plot device when Marge finds them in Tom's apartment in Venice, confirming her growing suspicions about Tom and almost leading to her own murder which is prevented by the appearance of her friend, Peter Smith-Kingsley (Jack Davenport). It is ironic that the rings assist Tom later when his possession of them is interpreted by Herbert Greenleaf as key evidence in support of the theory that Dickie committed suicide after murdering Freddie.

After Freddie's murder, Tom moves to Venice where he becomes attracted to Peter Smith-Kingsley, an open homosexual with whom Tom can relax. Their similar costuming, in casual, black sweaters, indicates their compatibility and the possibility of Tom carving out a new, confident and open identity as himself rather than as a 'fake' Dickie. With Peter there is no need for Tom to wear elaborate, initialled clothing in order to feel secure. The stark minimalism of their dress contrasts with Tom's previous outfits. The colour black is a signifier of the fashionable art-world of the 1950s, but it is also a portent of tragedy. On the boat at the end of the film, Tom wears Peter's black duffle coat and we think that the cycle of murder has finished, but the appearance of Meredith traps Tom into perpetuating the fantasy of being Dickie one more time, which necessitates Peter's murder. This is a different ending from both the novel and *Plein Soleil*: in the novel Peter, an incidental character, does not have a relationship with Tom, and Tom gets away with the murders; in *Plein Soleil* Peter does not feature at all and Tom is picked-up by the police when Dickie's body is discovered.

The expansion of Peter's role by Minghella is significant in that it suggests the possibility of happiness and peace for Tom, which is

Figure 4: Freddie (Philip Seymour Hoffman), Dickie (Jude Law), and Tom (Matt Damon) in his corduroy jacket, in *The Talented Mr Ripley*.

presented as never quite attainable when he is masquerading as Dickie. Minghella's decision not to let Tom sail away with Peter into the sunset is rather puzzling in view of the hitherto positive representation of their relationship and the precedent in Highsmith's novel of Tom getting away with two murders. The ending is, of course, predictable in moralistic terms – why should a murderer be rewarded with happiness – but also in terms of the film's exploration of the theme of identity. As such, identity is never stable, always in process and never quite able to escape the past. Tom's stability with Peter is then only as secure as the moment and Tom is never able to shake off Dickie's shadow.

With further reference to Lacan, the similarity of Tom and Peter's dress reminds us of the dressing-up scene when Tom posed as Dickie, experiencing a moment of *jouissance* that is immediately shattered by the reminder, through Dickie's interruption, of its inherent instability and transitory nature. Similarly, Meredith's presence on the boat jolts Tom into believing that his happiness with Peter is illusory, necessitating another murder of a love-object. A key difference this time is that his love has been reciprocated: love and desire have therefore been lost.

The theme of identity is explored with several other characters in *The Talented Mr Ripley* and as with Tom, costume is a key signifier. Dickie is searching for an identity which separates him from his father, New York and the family shipyards. In Highsmith's novel it is a not so much a case of what he wears but how he wears it, his aristocratic bearing/body determining his confident persona: 'He looked unusual with his long, finely cut face, his quick intelligent eyes, the proud way be carried himself regardless of what he was wearing. He was wearing broken-down sandals and rather soiled white pants now, but he sat there as if he owned the Galleria'. In *Plein Soleil*, Tom and Philippe are dressed similarly, but with small differences to emphasize Philippe's class and wealth, for example his good quality loose, casual clothing which is just that little bit more distinctive than Tom's. Since this film is concerned to present Tom as an impersonator whose murder of Philippe, as in the novel, is pre-meditated, the similarity between the two men is an important way to prepare the audience for the masquerade. Contrasting costumes are not therefore such a feature as in Minghella's film in which Dickie's outfits are a crucial indicator of his personality, charisma, identity, wealth and social status.

Dickie's wardrobe is a spectacular feature in *The Talented Mr Ripley*. His clothes are fashionable and chic, including white loafers, winklepickers, smart Italian-cut jackets and tailored lightweight casual shirts. In the film they are impeccable, which is in keeping with filmic representations of costumes from a particular period: an excess of chic is privileged over any attempt at realism in the sense that the clothes always look brand new. The film is set in 1958-9, the 'Il Boom' period, imbued with the spirit of *La Dolce Vita* (Frederico Fellini, 1960) and the Italian fascination with jazz. Italy's recovery after the Second World War was paving the way for affluence, if only confined to the rich, and saw the development of a youth culture centred around jazz clubs and coffee bars. Italian menswear was particularly distinctive in this period and Rome, where Tom and Dickie travel for jazz and fashion, was the most important centre for style and the location of top tailoring firms Brioni, Domenico, Caraceni, Duetti and Tornato (see Mendes and De la Haye 1999: 173). Early on in their acquaintance, Dickie and Tom walk along the streets of Mongibello and Dickie is beautifully dressed in a black shirt and dark grey jacket, wearing white loafers without socks. By contrast Tom is wearing green/brown colours, not to distract from the spectacle of Dickie's fashionable attire. Later, when Tom is wearing the much-maligned corduroy jacket, Dickie is dressed in an exquisitely tailored dark blue suit with a pork-pie hat which costume designer Ann Roth describes as Dickie's 'symbol of hipness: it says that the life he leads is not that of his father' (quoted in Hodgkinson 2000: 6). Neither is it that of Tom. Anthony Minghella intended to liken Dickie to a satyr (one of a class of Greek woodland deities in human form – used to indicate lust or sensuality), particularly with his short, white cotton trousers which show his calves (which also feature in *Plein Soleil*), his quick gestures and lithe body (as he discusses in the commentary included in the DVD release). As indicated in Highsmith's novel, Dickie's ease with himself is expressed in the way he wears casual, loose-fitting clothes made from soft fabrics which emphasize his body movements. Tom often wears shirts with stiffer collars and looks awkward by comparison, not at ease with himself or able to flaunt his body with such confidence.

This presentation of Dickie as the epitome of 'cool' makes us understand Tom's attraction for him and the lifestyle he enjoys. Instead of making Dickie a talentless painter, as in the novel, Minghella turns him into a charismatic musician who is knowledgeable about Blue Note jazz artists, including Chet Baker and Sonny Rollins. In *Plein Soleil* Philippe's yacht is called 'Marge', whereas in Minghella's film it is named 'Bird' in homage to jazz saxophonist Charlie Parker. Dickie's self-immersion into the exciting, volatile and frenetic world of jazz is an expression of his rebellion against his father, but in so doing he is creating an enviable world which is also based on privilege, but of a slightly different nature. This is perhaps where the elements of class critique are softened as Dickie's world is presented as desirable, fashionable, modern and sexual whereas in fact it is only possible for him to function within it as the son of a millionaire. Dickie's world contains snobbish distinctions of its own, however, which the audience is made aware of through identification with Tom's point of view. These are indicated by Dickie and Freddie's comments about Tom's jacket and the occasions when Tom is made painfully aware that members of the upper-class identify him as an outsider when, for example, they express incredulity that he has no skiing or sailing experience. Yet for all this there is an element of creativity about Dickie in his tasteful wardrobe, beautiful house, playing the saxophone, which is missing entirely from Philippe in *Plein Soleil* in which he shows no respect for Marge's writing, throwing her manuscript overboard the yacht and giving Tom a condescending lecture on how to hold a fish-knife. Even though Tom acquires a flair for jazz very quickly in *The Talented Mr Ripley,* it is Dickie who takes him to the best venues and has an infectious enthusiasm for the music, whereas we know that Tom's true preferences lie with classical music. The casting of Jude Law is also instrumental in making Dickie compelling, more so than any other character in the film. Even though we learn that he made an Italian woman pregnant and refused to give her money for an abortion, we never quite think he deserves such a violent death at the hands of Tom. In large part this response is structured by the seductive Italian milieu and Dickie's glamorous persona which is intimately related to the way he is dressed.

The women's costumes in *The Talented Mr Ripley* are equally as fascinating as the men's. As previously noted, Marge (Gwyneth Paltrow) is far more interesting in Minghella's version than she was in Highsmith's novel or in *Plein Soleil*. As Minghella explains, her character becomes more mature as the film progresses, from her scenes in Italy to her arrival in Rome and Venice (DVD commentary). This process can be measured in terms of her costuming. In Mongibello she wears comfortable clothes – bright patterned cotton skirts, white shirts tied at the waist, comfortable cardigans – not as immediately fashionable as Dickie's but reflective of her relaxed style and holiday mood. As the thriller elements of the plot develop after Dickie's murder, however, she appears to mature into an intelligent society woman, with her hair up and dressed in expensive clothes which invest her with a professional, elegant, and aristocratic demeanour. When she meets Dickie's father in Rome, she is wearing a leopardskin fitted coat and matching pillbox hat and later she appears in an elegant Norman Norrell dress and girdle, looking very sophisticated. The matching of costume to her growing significance in the plot means that we take her seriously as the only person who guesses the truth about Tom but who is silenced by the men around her: Dickie's father and the American detective who see no further than their limited interpretation of the case. Minghella likens Marge during the final scenes of the film to Grace Kelly, an appropriate inspiration as a woman who knows too much (DVD commentary).

Marge's clothes can be contrasted with those worn by Meredith Logue, who is extremely fashionable throughout the film. Meredith does not appear in the novel nor in *Plein Soleil* but was created by Minghella for dramatic suspense. Tom introduces himself to her as Dickie on their first meeting when they both arrive in Italy. He meets her again in Rome, creating further dramatic tension as Tom is forced by circumstances to switch identities on several occasions, back to Tom when he is Dickie and vice-versa. The most striking example of this is when Meredith invites Tom (thinking he is Dickie) to the opera and in the interval he bumps into Marge and Peter and has to remove his rings and become Tom again in an instant. In an almost farcical situation, he has to revert to Dickie's persona when he re-joins Meredith, making an excuse to leave the building so that he does not run into Marge and Peter again. Unlike Marge, Meredith's character does not really change so her costumes are less serious, with a touch of flamboyance, involving berets, scarves swathed over her shoulder as she pops up at the most inopportune moments. She is highly fashionable, wearing long, Parisian designer coats and dramatic evening dresses but her costumes are less sophisticated than those worn by Marge in Rome and Venice. It is ironic that just as Tom and Peter are sailing to what we think is a new life, Meredith is also on the boat with her family, causing Tom to slip back into his Dickie impersonation when they meet and leading to Peter's murder. Lacking the weight of character granted to Marge, Meredith is, however, crucial for an understanding of the ending which Minghella has constructed for the film. As previously argued, Meredith is the 'other' who interrupts Tom's momentary experience of unified bliss with Peter. It is an ending which endorses the instability of identity as Tom kills the only person in the narrative who accepts him for 'himself'.

Although many films deal with questions of identity, Highsmith's novel provided a particularly fascinating text which René Clément, Anthony Minghella and their respective costume designers, developed for the screen. This analysis of the different ways in which costume can be used to explore the theme of identity in these texts has shown that clothes can be read on many levels: as instruments of plot development; as 'signs' of character and personality; as accomplices in the creation of an overall 'look' and visual style of a film; and as evidence for the application of theoretical concepts, in this case Lacanian psychoanalysis, in the interpretation of film texts. In the under-researched area of the depiction of male fashion in films, both *Plein Soleil* and *The Talented Mr Ripley* illustrate the paradoxical way that costume can uncover many layers of meaning, as demonstrated by the analysis of the versions of Tom dressing in Dickie's clothes, positioning himself in front of various mirrors.

Reading films 'through the clothes' does not mean that other elements are insignificant, which is why analyses of costume should always reference the use of accessories and include a discussion of the overall setting. In *The Talented Mr Ripley,* Minghella placed his actors and their costumes in a blaze of sunlight and stunning scenery which one could argue is akin to the seductive charms of the mise-en-scène of the heritage film. Placed in a thriller context, however, the costumes and setting create a vivid contrast to 'the rather purgatorial journey that we are being led on' (Minghella in *American Cinematographer*, Jan 2000: 57), less of a holiday and more of a shattering experience. At the risk of softening the critique of class, Minghella's decision to make Dickie and Marge's world a showcase for Italian fashions and something of a nostalgic homage to *La Dolce Vita*, elaborated the sartorial descriptions which Highsmith considered to be crucial for an understanding of Tom's obsession with Dickie. In so doing, a distinctive adaptation has been produced which enables layers of subtext to become more visible and for the homosexual theme in particular to be explored in a more extensive manner than was possible in 1955 or in 1960.

3   DESPERATELY SEEKING SUSAN: TEXTURES OF TRANSFORMATION

> Susan was a queen of street-style trash whose wardrobe mirrored Madonna's lace and rosaries, sun glasses, stockings and suspenders. [...] On her first concert tour, Madonna was amazed to see the over-whelming influence her style was having on American youth culture. Hundreds of thousands of young girls came to the concerts dressed just like her, with bleached and tousled hair, see-through tops, bras, fingerless gloves and crucifixes (Voller 1992: 21).

Desperately Seeking Susan (Susan Seidelman, 1985) serves as an excellent case study for the impact of stardom on film costuming. In 1985, when the film was released, Madonna was emerging as an international pop star with a clearly defined 'street-style trash' look which Santo Loquasto, the production designer for *Desperately Seeking Susan*, exploited to the full. Susan was the epitome of what Madonna represented: street-wise, irreverent and subversive femininity. 'Like A Virgin', her controversial single and album, had been released towards the end of 1984 and established her reputation as a daring, seductive and original performer. Her transformation of 'ordinary' items such as lingerie into brazen expressions of non-conformity reflected dress practices which were associated with punk subculture. As Dick Hebdige

(1979) demonstrated by his semiotic analysis of *punk**, a *subcultural style** is created when items which are usually associated with safety, conservatism and repression are used in a radical way and in so doing generate new meanings which are expressive of an alternative lifestyle. Madonna's use of the corset and the crucifix, for example, can be interpreted as a subversive and parodic appropriation of mainstream culture. As a means of expanding the popularity of a relatively new star, *Desperately Seeking Susan*, arguably Madonna's best film performance, was a key element in establishing her persona which was defined in large part by her clothes. Assessing the impact of the film on 'street' clothing is, however, difficult, since Madonna's image was already in circulation. The film amplified what was being disseminated elsewhere.

With its central narrative about Roberta (Rosanna Arquette), a conservative, middle-class housewife, who becomes fascinated with Susan (Madonna), a rebellious, assertive drifter whose name she first encounters when reading the 'personals', *Desperately Seeking Susan* invites identification with Roberta's quest to meet Susan and undergo a physical and emotional transformation, eventually rejecting her former identity. Via a series of rather improbable events, Roberta is transported into a world which is diametrically opposed to her safe, suburban lifestyle. The central narrative of what Jackie Stacey calls 'feminine fascination' (1988: 115) provides ample scope for costume to become a central agency for both plot and characterization, aligning a mid-1980s audience with Roberta in their desire to imitate Susan/Madonna just at the time when she was becoming a major star. The film therefore provides an invitation for 'embodiment', the copying and personal adaptation of a star's clothes, and in so doing offers a playful but significant exploration of codes of femininity.

This chapter will use *Desperately Seeking Susan* as an example of the function of costume and accessories in a 'classic' text in which clothes are used in a fairly obtrusive manner. The film deploys a set of basic structural oppositions, as outlined by Graeme Turner (1988: 167):

Roberta	Susan
conventional	unconventional
bourgeois	anti-bourgeois
suburban	urban
married	unmarried
sexually submissive	sexually aggressive
boring	exciting
constrained	free

Desperately Seeking Susan involves a woman's journey of self-discovery, motivated by a series of questions which are resolved by the end of the narrative: how/will Roberta eventually meet her idol, Susan? What happens when Roberta becomes involved in Susan's world? What, if anything, do two women from completely different backgrounds have in common? How does the tension between the film's structural opposi- tions create a dynamic and compelling narrative? In analysing these key questions costume plays a key role as a means of advancing the plot and in suggesting the mutability of female identity, the possibility of transformation. As an adaptation of Madonna's image and persona for a fictional story, there is much to be observed in the film about the use of colours, clothes and accessories at a particular moment, the mid-1980s. With its theme of identity it also provides an interesting comparison with *The Talented Mr Ripley* which, as we have seen, deals with a case of masculine fascination from a different generic perspective.

Susan's distinctive short jacket with its gold pyramid design on the back, almost completely surrounded by a bright red, three-quarter circle and with lapels decorated with a wavy gold and black pattern, is a pivotal plot device. It is a classic *Hitchcockian McGuffin** which provides a literal and symbolic link between Susan and Roberta. We first see it after being introduced to Susan in an Atlantic City hotel room which she occupied with a man called Bruce. We later find out that just after Susan left the room Bruce was murdered by Richard Nolan, his blond jewel-thief accomplice, who saw Susan from behind as she left the room, the jacket being clearly visible. The jacket is thus established as the mechanism for his subsequent quest to recover the stolen Egyptian earrings which he believes are in its pocket. Since he did not see Susan's face he chases whoever wears the jacket, bringing danger to Roberta when she is mistaken for Susan. This escalates after Roberta follows Susan into a second-hand shop where she swaps the jacket for a pair of boots and leaves quickly so Roberta loses sight of her. Disappointed, Roberta buys the jacket, puts it on and begins to get drawn into Susan's world.

The plot continues to be inextricably linked to the fate of the jacket. Susan's boyfriend, Jim, asks his friend Dez to look out for Susan at Battery Park, telling him that she wears a jacket with a pyramid on the back. Since Dez does not know Susan he mistakes Roberta for her because of the jacket. Similarly, Nolan chases after her when he sees her wearing the jacket. As she is chased she collides with a post as Dez comes to her rescue. The blow to Roberta's head causes her to lose her memory so Dez assumes that she is Susan, an identity which she is unable to challenge since she cannot remember who she is. She finds a key in the jacket pocket which Dez recognises as belonging to a Port Authority locker which they discover holds Susan's large bag which contains one of the stolen earrings. In an extremely convoluted manner, the jacket has thus facilitated what would otherwise be an extremely improbable instance of Roberta being mistaken for Susan. It becomes a sort of stand-in for Susan, an authentication of her presence which Roberta wants to remember. As Laura Mulvey has observed: 'When Susan disappears, she bequeaths, as it were, a magical object to Roberta, the jacket which fills the gap left by her absence. The jacket will provide the means of transporting Roberta into the other world where she in turn will get caught up in danger and romance by temporarily "becoming" Susan' (1998: 127).

As such, the jacket is a simple but effective device to bring the characters together and to link the story of the stolen earrings with

Figure 5: Susan (Madonna) wearing the pyramid jacket in *Desperately Seeking Susan*.

Roberta's quest to find out more about Susan. With its pyramid motif it is also symbolic of another world, the world of exoticism and excitement which Roberta associates with Susan, travel, romance and adventure. As an item of clothing the jacket is Roberta's *aide-mémoire** of Susan. Although they have never met, Roberta has seen her and buys the jacket as a reminder of her adventure when, after reading Jim's message to Susan in 'the personals', she went to Battery Park to see Susan meet Jim. It therefore stands in for the lifestyle she craves but which appears to be directly opposite to her experience as a housewife. The jacket itself is an object of mystery: Susan tells the proprietor of the second-hand shop that the jacket belonged to Jimi Hendrix, thus investing it with a radical heritage but when he sells it to Roberta, the proprietor assesses her different background from her appearance and says that it belonged to Elvis Presley. It is invested with yet another meaning when Roberta returns home and her husband, Gary, is puzzled by her purchase, amazed that she bought second-hand goods, commenting, 'What, are we poor?' He cannot understand why she would want to purchase it whereas we know that for her it represents the non-acquisitive values of excitement and independence and a temporary loss of responsibility: she was so caught up with her quest to see Susan that she forgot the errand her husband asked her to do when she was in town.

Paradoxically, the pyramid motif also relates to the design on dollar bills, creating a further intertextual link with Madonna's world as a 'Material Girl', the title of one of her records. From this perspective, the jacket can be read as acknowledgement of Madonna's place as instigator of capitalist consumerism (in Marxist terms, *commodity fetishism**), noted by E. Ann Kaplan (1990). Similarly, in the film narrative, Susan is resourceful and street-wise, taking care of herself, stealing money from Bruce and refusing to pay for taxis. This is somewhat ironic since whereas for Roberta and Susan the jacket is mysterious and glamorous, for Gary it does nothing to show off his wealth in the classic sense that Veblen described female clothes as a demonstration of bourgeois wealth and social aspiration (1899/1953). The jacket also leads to Susan meeting-up with Gary, Roberta's husband, when she returns to the second-hand shop to recover the jacket, learns that it has been bought and leaves her telephone number in case it is returned. Remembering that Roberta had bought a second-hand jacket, Gary recognises the shop's distinctive carrier bag in his kitchen and when he goes there to investigate Roberta's disappearance he is given Susan's number by the proprietor. Another improbable meeting is therefore facilitated by the use of the jacket as it propels the plot via its encounters with the various characters.

The Egyptian earrings perform a similar function in the film as valuable jewels which get separated at the beginning when Susan wears one and leaves the other in the bag which she deposits in the Port Authority locker, to be recovered by Roberta and Dez. The two earrings are reunited at the end of the film when Roberta and Susan eventually meet and are treated as heroines for recovering the stolen jewellery. In the original ending of the film which was cut after preview screenings, Susan and Roberta are last seen riding camels in the desert, the implication being that they have left everything behind, including their respective men. Unusually, in this film the desert and Egyptian symbols (the earrings and the pyramid on the jacket) represent female self-discovery. It is interesting to consider how this offers an alternative perspective to the final frames of the released version in which Roberta ends up with Dez and Susan with Jim. In opposition to the more conventional heterosexual couplings it could be argued that the original ending places the women's relationship far more centrally as the desired closure, which would be supported by knowledge of Madonna's bisexuality. The separation and subsequent recovery of the earrings are therefore symbolic of the two women's gradual journey towards each other, even if this is perhaps not so clearly expressed in the released version of the film.

Costume is used to connote differences between the two women and the worlds they represent from the beginning. Much of the film's narrative pleasure resides with its exploration of the unlikely convergence of two different lifestyles, indicating that it is possible to reject an affluent but unhappy existence and that self-fulfillment and self-worth need not necessarily be related either to convention or material gain. Colour is the primary device which is used to juxtapose the two opposing ways of life, middle-class conservatism and counter-culture. In the opening sequence we are introduced to Roberta in a beauty parlour. The predominant pastel colours are shades of pink and warm oranges as we see the women being given various beauty treatments. In keeping with classical texts which introduce women 'in bits', the first shot is of a woman's leg receiving hair-remover treatment, followed by a close-up of a foot having its toe-nails painted red and then we see a hand being used as a tester for different shades of lipstick. The emphasis is on controlled transformation, almost clinic-like, via the accoutrements of the beauty business as we are shown a row of women under hair driers, all wearing similar gowns, while others, like Roberta, are having their hair cut. It is interesting that Roberta is introduced to us from the back view so what we see is her reflection in the mirror as she talks to her stylist. The reflected image indicates that she is not yet complete, not the Roberta we will come to know, and this is a good visual indication of the narrative which follows. The emphasis is on her appearance being created for someone else's approval, since the style deemed appropriate for her by her sister-in-law and by the stylist is 'not weird', something her husband 'will love'. As her hair is being dried she reads the 'Desperately Seeking Susan' notice from Jim in the 'personals' and her fascination is obvious, her longing also to be 'desperate', which her sister-in-law dismisses with incredulity. Roberta circles the notice with nail varnish, allowing us to see the notice in detail but also making use of nail varnish in an unconventional way, a gesture which is repeated by Susan in the next sequence.

The beauty parlour sequence ends abruptly with an establishing shot of a hotel in Atlantic City and the film's title is displayed as we are prepared for our first sight of Susan. Susan inhabits a completely different environment and is coded as a 'modern', liberated woman. The music changes from a girl-group 1960s pop song ('The Shoop Shoop Song' in the US version, 'One Fine Day' in the UK version) to a raunchy, thumping beat accompanied by the brassy tones of a saxophone as we see inside the hotel room where Susan has been staying with Bruce. The colours of the room are much stronger – floor-length red curtains with the debris of the previous night's passionate encounter fully in evidence – than the pastel shades of the beauty parlour as we see Susan lying on the floor taking a Polaroid photograph of herself. This indicates vanity, exhibitionism and self-confidence which we subsequently identify with her character. We also, of course, recognize her as Madonna since the outfit she wears resembles the costumes she wore on stage in the mid-1980s, and the attitude of the character Susan immediately replicates Madonna's own outrageous persona. In contrast to Roberta she is dressed in black leggings and a tight, low-cut top, wearing the pyramid jacket and festooned with with elaborate, dangling jewellery including the crucifix that had become an integral aspect of Madonna's 'look' in 1985. Instead of being introduced 'in bits' we see the whole person lying on the floor in a hedonistic pose which identifies her as an exhibitionist and star. The jacket with the pyramid on the back is made clear to us as she reads the notice from Jim in the paper and like Roberta marks it, but this time in the shape of a heart with her eye pencil. This gesture is another instance of an implied connection between the two women, so it is appropriate that while they have been introduced to us as very different people, as their destinies are to become intertwined they resort to the same method of marking the notice by using make-up. As Turner has observed: 'This alternating narrative movement establishes what Susan, Roberta and their respective worlds might be like and what they might mean, by carefully depicting those worlds. All the systems of signification work to construct a network of difference and similarity between the contexts and the characters' (1988: 169-70).

Susan packs her bag which is large and round-shaped with a black and white skull pattern (which we later see painted on Jim's van). The bag holds her possessions, including one of the earrings which she takes while Bruce is asleep. She puts on the other one and leaves the room after stealing Bruce's money. As an accessory, the bag is significant in that it is large enough to hold all Susan needs to travel, and as she leaves the hotel room the camera focuses on it in a shot which is similar to Hitchcock's famous opening of *Marnie* (1964) which tracks a woman's handbag from behind as she walks down a railway platform. *Marnie* is about a woman who steals to be independent and frequently changes her identity by using forged social security cards which she keeps in her bag and by changing her hair colour. As a single woman, Susan, like Marnie, has control of her handbag and is independent of male authority, in contrast to Roberta. As I have argued elsewhere, this is a classic Hitchcockian way of using a handbag, a woman's private space, to represent female assertiveness and independence (1995: 23-37). The bag also functions as a symbol of Susan's control over her sexuality: she leaves Bruce to meet Jim. As a plot device it is important because it bursts open in the hotel corridor so that Susan has to bend down to shut it, thus revealing the back of her jacket in an obtrusive way to Nolan, the mobster who passes her on his way to Bruce's room.

The next sequence is of a party at Roberta and Gary's house which contrasts sharply with the introduction of Susan. The colours are again predominantly pastel. Roberta's pink dress is long and silky and she is wearing her hair up. The guests are dressed similarly, giving the impression of a comfortable suburban middle-class life, as they watch a commercial on television advertising Gary's spa tubs, 'Gary's Oasis', which is preceded by a news item about stolen Egyptian artefacts, providing a plot link with the previous sequence. As Roberta gazes out of the window at the bridge between New Jersey and Manhattan, with the sound of the advertisement in the background as it ends with the auspicious words 'all your fantasies can come true', a link is forged with the next sequence of Susan arriving in New York, travelling over the bridge by bus from Atlantic City. The linking music is also suggestive of transformation and longing, creating a connection between the two women before they have ever met.

After Susan leaves the bus she goes to the subway and is wearing a sleeveless pink top, trousers with braces and long beads. In keeping with her previous presentation as a carefree, street-wise, independent woman she takes advantage of the subway facilities as if they were her own bathroom, as she uses the hand-drying machine to dry her armpits without a hint of self-consciousness. Again, in a scene which is similar to one which occurs near the beginning of *Marnie*, we see her place her large bag in a Port Authority locker, putting the key in the pocket of the pyramid jacket. When Roberta later collects the bag with Dez she becomes its new owner, taking on a temporary identity as Susan, with her amnesia providing the plot device for her disappearance from home and the beginning of her adventures as being mistaken for Susan. The bag has therefore proved to be a crucial accessory in advancing the plot and in suggesting the assertive and resourceful nature of Susan's femininity.

Roberta's entry into Susan's milieu occasions many interesting costume changes. Small touches are important, for example when she collects the bag from the locker she is wearing red cowboy boots which are symbolic of her discovery of a latent, more liberated identity, creating an intertextual association with *The Wizard of Oz* (Victor Fleming, 1939) in which Dorothy's red shoes similarly indicate transformation. Gone are the pastel colours and tasteful cardigans as Roberta proudly wears the pyramid jacket and later she puts on Susan's green lamé dress which she found in the bag. As a pivotal facilitator of plot, the bag also contains a card for the Magic Club which she visits in search of a clue to jolt her memory but where she ends up being given a job. For her act at the Magic

Club she wears a pink tutu and later is mistaken for a prostitute when she is still wearing it outside the club. Whereas the pastel shades of her former costume indicated middle-class respectability the pink tutu, worn in combination with the jacket and a wig, invests her with a far more dangerous, risqué image. This contrast is further elaborated when Gary and his sister discover that Roberta has been arrested and Gary's sister concludes that she must have been leading a double life as a prostitute or lesbian.

The incongruity of her former image with her present predicament is exploited to the full but it is noticeable that she maintains an innocent demeanour throughout. The audience has superior knowledge of the 'true' Roberta who, as Stacey points out, is marked by her difference from Susan on many occasions, despite her wilder appearance (1988: 128-9). Although their paths and lifestyles become increasingly convergent, their personalities are not the same. Such nuances are indicated by the overall impact of Roberta in her new outfits: again, not so much what she wears but *how* she wears her new-found wardrobe. With her finer bone structure, even when Roberta's clothes that are similar to Susan's, she never looks quite as wild or carefree. In her exchanges with Dez she does not behave as he expects from Susan, never quite throwing off her placatory and mild demeanour. The final outfit we see Roberta wearing is perhaps a compromise – a long, dark green, narrow-lapelled jacket which is in complete contrast to her costume at the beginning of the film but nevertheless preserves an elegant quality. As a character, Roberta changes more than Susan but never quite convinces as a punk or as a stand-in for Susan. With their respective characters and costumes Roberta and Susan have therefore represented different facets of 'the feminine'.

The similarity between Susan's clothes and those made fashionable by Madonna has already been noted, but it is striking how *Desperately Seeking Susan* utilizes her image on many occasions. When Susan is in prison for not paying a taxi fare, she is wearing a typical outfit which came to be associated with Madonna's 'look': black leggings, a bare midriff, a black lacy top with a clearly visible black bra underneath. When she sits beside her friend outside the Magic Club they both wear brightly-coloured outfits; Susan in a vivid red top, orange socks, long black gloves and the silver sequined boots she exchanged for the jacket. These are similar to Madonna's stage outfits which facilitated many merchandizing promotions. At one time Macy's in New York devoted an entire floor to 'Madonnaland', selling Madonna-like clothes, jewellery and posters. The impact of her 'look' could even be discerned in the designs of couturiers such as Christian Lacroix at the house of Pitou and Karl Lagerfield at Chanel (Voller 1992: 22). As a box-office success the film extended Madonna's popularity overseas, particularly in the United Kingdom where the punk look had already been adapted from the US music scene and popularised in the UK by Malcolm McLaren and Vivienne Westwood. Madonna's appropriation of religious symbols, such as the crucifix, flaunted a subcultural style which many interpreted as irreverent. The extent to which such iconographic elements of her emerging star persona are included in the film is striking. It is also significant, in seeing the film as a star vehicle, to note that even though Madonna had far fewer lines than Rosanna Arquette she nevertheless occupied a 'privileged image as glamour' (Mulvey 1998: 127). To intensify this effect the cinemagrapher, Ed Lachman, explained that even when on the move Madonna was shot with a much tighter framing strategy than that used for Arquette. As Mulvey goes on to observe, this strategy 'intensifies Madonna's construction as image – in close-up and to a certain extent removed from the normal rules of continuity shooting. At times she appears almost like a silent star, with the full force of cinematic glamour invested in her image'.

Desperately Seeking Susan demonstrates, however, a nuanced deployment of Madonna's star image which predominates for most of the film but which is not always essential for the advancement of the plot. When, for example, Susan visits Gary's house, it is noticeable that the character of Susan becomes more prominent than Madonna in that Roberta's world can be seen to affect what she wears, if only on a temporary basis. While the technique of wearing underwear as outerwear is utilized when she lounges on the bed reading Roberta's diary, the colours are much lighter and the fabrics softer than we have seen in her previous costuming. One conclusion is that the two women are perhaps not so dissimilar and that their rendezvous is inevitable. Costume is used to anticipate future intimate exchanges of friendship when, knowing that Roberta was the person who bought the pyramid jacket, Susan takes one of Roberta's black sequined jackets from her wardrobe. The jacket is one which would have looked smart with one of Roberta's 'hostess' outfits but when worn by Susan is invested with a more subversive look. The exchange of jackets is thus symbolic of the two women's increasingly convergent paths and of Roberta's escape from her stifling marriage.

The male characters in the film also wear interesting costumes. Jim wears punk clothing – black sleeveless t-shirts, tight trousers and leathery, textured jackets. His style is 'street' fashion, fitting in with his work in a punk band. Not so much a part of the punk world, Dez is dressed in loose, dark trousers and dark t-shirts with braces. While his clothes are fairly unremarkable they become more significant when contrasted with Gary's conventional attire – beige, lightweight suits. The differences in male costumes are highlighted most obviously in the scene when Gary meets Susan at a club. He looks extremely conservative and out of place – loosening up for him means unfastening his tie as he dances awkwardly with Susan. When we see him at home he wears 'leisurewear', soft, comfortable but profoundly unstylish clothes which are made from soft fabrics and in pastel colours. As with the women's clothes, extremes of appearance are demonstrated, indicating both social differences and representations of 'the masculine'. Whereas Jim and Dez are portrayed as tolerant 'new men', Gary is caricatured as an up-tight man who limits his wife's choices and refuses to believe that she might want to be independent.

As two films which have examined questions of identity from different generic perspectives, it is interesting to compare *The Talented Mr Ripley* (psychological thriller) with *Desperately Seeking Susan* (screwball comedy/women's film). There are similarities between the two: both films deal with characters, Tom and Roberta respectively, who become fascinated by another person of their own sex, Dickie and Susan. The first glimpse of the 'desired one' is strikingly similar in the two films as both Tom and Roberta see the object of their fascination through glasses. From his hotel Tom spies Dickie and Marge diving off the boat through binoculars and Roberta sees Susan meet Jim through a pay-slot telescope at Battery Park. These shots encourage the audience to identify with the pursuers' fascination and, as Stacey has pointed out in relation to *Desperately Seeking Susan*, these same-sex looks transgress the traditional gender positionalities of classic narrative cinema (1988: 126). Both films also use a jacket as a key element of plot – the Princeton jacket and the association of Tom with his corduroy jacket in *The Talented Mr Ripley* and the pyramid jacket in *Desperately Seeking Susan*. These garments, however, exceed the demands of plot by also symbolising complex issues of identity in connection with the respective characters' desires. In *The Talented Mr Ripley,* the Princeton jacket represents Tom's wish to be upwardly-mobile, to be entitled to the riches and social acceptance it confers on its wearer, to make him feel a 'somebody'. As such it prefigures the rest of the story which uses clothes to contrast his existence as 'ordinary' Tom in his corduroy jacket, with his post-murder masquerade as privileged Dickie, for whom doors are opened and people wait on attendance. In the scene analysed in the previous chapter when Tom tries on Dickie's clothes in front of a mirror, his desire to look like his 'ideal' is expressed primarily through costume. While not really suggesting homosexual desire to the same extent as in *The Talented Mr Ripley*, *Desperately Seeking Susan* uses the jacket to symbolise Roberta's identification with Susan and as an agent of transformation for her own life. With its Egyptian symbolism, however, it could also be argued that it supports the perhaps sexually ambiguous implications of the original ending of the film when Susan and Roberta are seen riding camels in the desert. In this instance the desert indicates their freedom, an opting out of convention. It is a space where the two women can be mobile and active, upsetting the more typical association of the desert with masculine identity, such as in *Lawrence of Arabia* (David Lean, 1962).

Both *The Talented Mr Ripley* and *Desperately Seeking Susan* deal with questions of identity in the first instance through difference. Tom's appearance is frequently contrasted with Dickie's and, as the analysis of the opening sequence of *Desperately Seeking Susan* has shown, Roberta's beauty-parlour world of soft pinks and 'not weird' styles is pitted against Susan's gritty, brash, punk appearance which is expressed by her distinctive black clothes, wild hairstyle and heavy jewellery, and is aurally punctuated by the thudding drum beats of the soundtrack. As both films develop, however, their characters develop similarities, especially when the device of mistaken identity is deployed. Nevertheless, even when Tom and Roberta are mistaken, for very different reasons, for their idols, they still maintain an element of difference, despite their respective masquerades. Tom as Dickie maintains an aspect of Tom's rather up-tight personality – he is far from the quixotic satyr portrayed so well by Jude Law. His clothes are also more formal – elegant suits rather than the loose but chic shirts worn by Dickie. Similarly, when Roberta has amnesia and is mistaken for Susan by Dez she does not emerge as a convincing Susan, an impression which is reinforced by the film's cinematographic style which clearly privileges Madonna as a dynamic star.

It would appear, therefore, that both films offer complex and nuanced studies of masculine and feminine identities revealing, through their costuming, a wide spectrum of difference, fluidity and possibility. Other films that feature same-sex clothes-swapping also suggest the surface elements of identity. As Stella Bruzzi has demonstrated in her analysis of *Single White Female* (Barbet Schroeder, 1992), in a noir/thriller context, 'the horror lies ... in the ease with which one character can pass for another' (1997: 143). In this film, one female character's obsessional and sexually-charged desire to look (hence *be*) another, results in a pathological fascination that gets out of control. The film provides a vivid representation of how clothing can disguise, confuse and destabilize notions that identity can be deciphered by appearance. Whereas *Desperately Seeking Susan* uses costume to assist Roberta's personal journey and transformation, implying that a change of image is healthy and self-fulfilling, *The Talented Mr Ripley* also explores a darker side in which the quest for 'true' identity is fraught with pain and even death.

This much less utopian interpretation of the consequences of radical or fraudulent changes in appearance is not entirely absent from *Desperately Seeking Susan* when, for example, Roberta is suspected of soliciting and is arrested because of the way she looks. As Annette Kuhn has observed in relation to the performative aspects of clothing: 'Far from being a fixed signifier of a fixed identity, clothing has the potential to disguise, to alter, even to reconstruct the wearer's self' (1985: 52). In this way both films demonstrate the positive and negative aspects of exploring a different identity, showing how dress can create a different impression, inspire confidence or be misinterpreted.

This sense of instability is reinforced by hindsight, when we understand that Madonna's image in *Desperately Seeking Susan* was merely one of her many 'phases' or 'looks', as part of her constantly mutating persona. As E. Ann Kaplan has pointed out, part of her fascination has been her refusal to remain 'fixed' into a stable identity: 'it is not a matter of locating an authentic Madonna core that can be extricated from the various wrappings that enclose her; rather, it is a question of peeling off layer after layer to reveal precisely the absence where a core might be' (1993: 150). In their different ways, *The Talented Mr Ripley*, Madonna and Susan therefore explore the often frustrating, but always intriguing and limitless possibilities, of transformation.

4   WONDERLAND: THE EMBODIMENT OF 'THE REAL'

Whereas the previous analyses have been of films which use costume in a spectacular way, as historical re-creation and as an indicator of social, gender and sexual identity, contemporary 'realist' films, which aim to convey something of life 'as it is', deploy similar and yet different methods of sartorial representation. This chapter will focus on Michael Winterbottom's *Wonderland* (1999) as an example of how films which deal with 'the real', that is, issues of everyday life, use costume to enhance their claim to realism, to persuade the audience that their observations relate to the complexities of reality.

As a concept, realism has been the subject of much debate (see Lapsley and Westlake 1988: 157-80) and among the various forms of realist text, *Wonderland* relates most closely to that which can be identified with aesthetic experiment. Winterbottom's use of naturalistic acting and manipulation of film form, with his frequent use of close-ups, speeded-up images and slow-motion, attempts to convey a sense of 'the real', of the imponderables of life. This tradition works in opposition to what Colin MacCabe (1974: 7-27) identified as the 'classic' realist text which, instead of making the audience aware of is construction sought to conceal its artifice, with the effect of closing off meaning. In an attempt to be convincing about its authenticity, a recognizable world could be conveyed by using techniques such as deep-focus photography, creating 'a window on the world'. As Graeme Turner has observed of the formal properties of the 'classic' realist text:

> The technologies of film production are hidden, so that techniques which might draw attention to the means of construction are kept to a minimum. Editing is as seamless as possible, the mise-en-scène is as dense as that of real life, camera movements tend to keep pace with the movement of the spectator's eyes, and perspective is maintained as if there were but one spectator (1988: 155).

In contrast, by using unconventional formal strategies, *Wonderland* seeks to convince by making its construction very apparent. The film is unashamed about its status as a cultural representation which uses costume to address in a textual form what Entwistle refers to as 'embodiment'. She writes that semiotic and textual analyses of costume frequently neglect the complexities of how people use fashion in relation to their bodies:

> The modern self is increasingly aware of itself, including its appearance, and able to intervene and act upon it. Classes and subcultures employ dress, body, posture and so on to create identity self-consciously both to affirm group affiliation and difference to those on the outside and within. Thus when talking about individuality and identity and the role played by fashion and dress it is important to recognize that identities are socially meaningful. The individual may want to 'stand out' but she or he also wants to 'fit in' with a group (2000: 139).

The 'situated practice' of wearing clothes is therefore a complex process of adaptation, negotiation and self-presentation. While sociological analyses attempt to explore the 'lived experience' of dress and fashion through use of surveys, interviews and other relevant methodologies, it would be a mistake to dismiss textual analysis as inappropriate for the task of studying 'situated practice'. As a close examination of the costumes in *Wonderland* shows, texts with an aesthetic approach to realism are able to suggest many of the nuances of 'embodiment' and elements of the social complexities referred to above by Entwistle. The realist imperative encourages a fashion system which is reflective of how 'ordinary' people use fashion, the different characters' relationships with each other, their social class, as well as punctuating narrative events in subtle ways. Although on first sight the costumes in *Wonderland* might therefore appear not to be as overtly significant as those in *Desperately Seeking Susan*, they nevertheless play an important role in exploring the various characters' identities and in facilitating social and cultural verisimilitude. It is also crucial to recognize that realist texts are no less subject to anachronism than non-realist texts. The aim of realist (and other) texts is to create a plausible link between a character and what they wear. As Julia Hallam explains, realist films use mise-en-scène as a fundamental means of establishing authenticity in which various 'modalities of referentiality are signified', including costume (2000: 102).

Wonderland examines one family's complex interrelationships over four days, Thursday to Sunday. Three sisters, Nadia (Gina McKee), Debbie (Shirley Henderson) and Molly (Molly Parker) live in London. Nadia, who describes herself in the beginning of the film as 'independent, honest, self-aware', is anxious to meet someone through 'lonely hearts' telephone advertising. Debbie, the oldest, is a 29-year-old hairdresser who lives alone with her young son, Jack, and Molly is expecting her first baby by her partner Eddie (John Simm). Their parents live nearby and we quickly learn that their marriage is difficult. The mother, Eileen, detests where she lives and is tormented by a dog which barks incessantly in the garden next door. They have a son, Darren, who has left London but whom we see on several occasions when he returns with a girlfriend, staying in a lavish hotel. The only contact he has with the family is when he leaves a message on his father's answerphone at the end of the film, letting them know that he is fine. Structured by the four days, the film charts Nadia's search for love; Debbie's sexual exploits and her conflict with Dan, Jack's father; Eddie's problems coming to terms with imminent fatherhood and the parents' stifling home life. The birth of Molly's baby at the end of the film relieves the bleakness of their respective stories. The final scenes produce a fairly optimistic closure as Eddie and Molly are brought together by their baby; Debbie is shown to be sensitive and caring with her son after he was mugged at a firework party; Eileen poisons the dog and so gets some peace; Darren's telephone call is welcomed by his father and Nadia walks off with Franklyn, the son of Donna, one of her parents' neighbours, the implication being that they will have a relationship.

Through these narrative strands the film explores the differences between the three sisters and costume is a key device in conveying style, personality and outlook. Nadia has a sense of fashion in whatever she wears. That is, her clothes are subject to her own particular 'system'; there are consistencies in what she wears and the director uses these to indicate aspects of her personality. When we first see her, she is in a crowded bar with one of her 'lonely hearts' dates, her hair up and wearing a patterned top which is made of very thin material so that we can see that she has a singlet on underneath. Apart from conveying fashion, this 'layered' look which we see her deploying on several subsequent occasions is perhaps symbolic, in this context, of her shyness, of the need for people to probe beneath her profoundly unconfident surface. When her date tells her that she 'looks great' she down-plays her sense of style by telling him that she bought the top because it was cheap. The clothes and their layers have therefore assisted in establishing character: Nadia's rather diffident, social awkwardness co-exists with her creative adaptation of bargain-basement clothes. The date does not go well and she leaves the pub alone, putting on a jacket and a small

Figure 6: Nadia (Gina McKee) in *Wonderland*.

rucksack made of shiny, synthetic material. It is triangular in shape
and has a gold and black pattern with a zip down the middle. We see
this rucksack on many subsequent occasions – it is her version of a
handbag. Hardly a safe item to be carrying on the London underground,
it is pure style and again indicative of Nadia's appearance contradicting
her manner. Winterbottom frequently films Nadia from behind so that we
get a clear image of the rucksack as she walks along the streets. Much of
his filming strategy concentrates on close-ups, but it is noticeable how
many times we are able to examine Nadia's 'layered' attire, this time a
black and grey hooded jacket with a dark blue t-shirt underneath. The
rucksack and hood can be read as signifiers of journeys and searching
which is appropriate for Nadia as she wanders the streets and travels on
the underground. Since much of Winterbottom's film is about displaying
the city, Nadia's journeys, punctuated either by speeded-up images

or slow-motion, intensify the sense of alienation found in postmodern cities (the slow-motion effects can be compared to Scorsese's similar use of the technique to express the human degradation of city life in *Taxi Driver* (1976)). People appear to merge into each other and become a nondescript blur of colour, as Xan Brooks has commented: 'Winterbottom's bittersweet course spirits us through a London that's positively awash with lost souls' (2000: 62). Nadia's attempt to adapt her clothes into a style which can be described as distinctive can thus be read as a classic case of costume being used to fix identity in a context of uncertainty. Her choice of layers is also symbolic of the multi-faceted nature of postmodern identity: they are an attempt to conceal her body but at the same time invest it with a sense of intrigue.

Debbie's clothes are very different but like Nadia she adapts them to create a particular image. She is more brash and confident than Nadia, projecting a persona of toughness, vibrancy and resilience. Debbie's identity is more overtly sexual and her clothes are tight-fitting, showing off her body. Our first sight of her is when she is at home with her son, Jack, and she is wearing a white, figure-hugging (although she is very slight), v-necked sweater with a mauve top underneath. Her clothes are expressive of her desire to be seen as sexually available, to play down her responsibilities as a mother. When she meets Nadia at the café where she works, Debbie suggests that they go out to a club and tells Nadia that she wants to buy a very tight, white lace top, 'size 6'. Later, we see her having sex in the salon where she works, totally in contol of the situation, enjoying the experience of being pleasured, and dancing afterwards in her bra, a black open shirt and a mauve, pencil skirt. Her partner asks her why she did not ask him home with her and she tells him about her son, giving the impression that although hedonistic she is careful about bringing men home. The tightness of her clothes and their sexualised nature is therefore reflective of the tension between pleasure and responsibility, responsibility not only for her son but also for her younger sister Molly who seems to rely on her a great deal. On other occasions she wears 'street-wise' clothes, black leggings, tight black tops and a short denim jacket which again fix her as a sharp, assertive young woman who refuses to become staid.

Clothes are used to create a link between the third sister, Molly, and her mother, Eileen. When we first see Molly she is wearing an over-shirt with a large check pattern and looks very obviously pregnant. Molly has on a much smarter red dress when her mother visits her, and when she goes to have her hair re-styled by Debbie she is also wearing clothes which have been chosen for the occasion – a smart striped shirt. When Eileen returns from visiting Molly, her neighbour, Donna, comments on her smart appearance. Donna is also smart: in this scene she wears a black jumper and a black and white leopard-skin patterned coat and her clothes are striking when later she welcomes Bill, Eileen's husband, into her house when he has locked himself out. On this occasion she is dressed in a black and white top with a short, seductive, almost transparent black skirt. She makes them cocktails and they dance together, suggesting a brief flirtation which he cuts short. By contrast, when Eileen is at home she is dressed in baggy clothes which appear to hide her body, in drab colours which underscore her depression. The morning after she has poisoned the dog, however, she has on a much brighter blue-and-pink-striped cardigan, as if she has dressed herself to mark the happy occasion of a quieter life. Both mother and daughter therefore use clothes to make themselves feel better, to remind them of different possibilities. This 'coupling' through costume is consistent with the film's investment in Molly as the bearer of hope for Eileen, leaving the audience with a perhaps less pessimistic impression of her life than has hitherto been suggested.

As with the female characters, costume is used to suggest differences between the men in *Wonderland*. Bill wears clothes that are perhaps the most bland: pale rainjackets, beige and grey pullovers which suggest a willingness to conform, to put up with a loveless marriage, which is supported by his abrupt exit from Donna's house. Eddie, Molly's

Figure 7: Molly (Molly Parker), Debbie (Shirley Henderson), and Nadia (Gina McKee in *Wonderland*.

husband, starts off in the film as a kitchen salesman and so we mostly see him in work clothes, a blue shirt and check tie. Interestingly, all the men wear some variation on this tie when they are seen at work, particularly Franklyn, Donna's son, who works in a hi-fi store and who otherwise has a sophisticated sense of dress. The 'uniform' of working life is not really experimented with at all, indicating far less creativity about clothes than we have seen with the women. The outfit which is associated most strikingly with Eddie is his scooter-gear. His rides occur at key moments in the film: after he has quit his job and when he fails to return home to discuss the situation with Molly when she has found out the truth. His accident on the scooter and subsequent hospitalisation create an opportunity for their reunion when Molly is in the same hospital having her baby. When Eddie rides his scooter we see many shots of him in his black helmet, shots which do not need to be in the film purely to advance the plot. As a related aspect of costume, a helmet is of course an interesting item because it obscures the face. The 'L' plate on his scooter, however, gives an indication of the vulnerability behind Eddie's 'armoured' appearance when wearing the helmet. In terms of Eddie's dilemma − whether he should persevere with a job which he hates because of the baby − it is expressive of his desire to abandon responsibility, to shut out the world. The plot punishes him for trying to do this by having him crash the scooter − he cannot escape fatherhood − but in a sense it also rewards him by creating the opportunity to reunite with Molly.

This device − a male character 'dressing up' to protect himself against the world − is also used with Jack who goes out on his own to a fireworks party wearing a rucksack and ear-plugs for his Walkman. In terms of the narrative this is a moving sequence because we know that he wanted to attend the fireworks with his mother who has had to accompany Molly to the hospital. Jack's father has gone out in search of a good time and left him on his own. The sight of the small boy walking to the fireworks party, protected, as it were, by his baggage and Walkman, is therefore all the more poignant since we empathise with his disappointment and fear for his vulnerability. Just as Eddie crashes when he thinks that his costume disguises his appearance, Jack is mugged and his bag and Walkman are stolen: no matter what accoutrements are used to conceal the body and create an impression of invulnerability, 'the self' is always in danger of exposure.

Debbie's ex-partner, Dan, is depicted as unreliable, thinking mostly of himself when taking his son out and leaving him on his own when he goes out to meet a 'lonely hearts' contact who turns out to be Nadia. We get the impression that he has made some money, driving a BMW and wearing a blue shirt and a fashionable beige suit made from ribbed material with wide, distinctive lapels which Nadia tells him looks 'splendid'. When she asks him where he bought it he refuses to be specific, rather like her down-playing of her outfit which was admired by her date in the first scene. The other male character who displays an interest in clothes is Nadia's admirer Franklyn, who we assume will become a greater part of her life at the end of the film. At work he wears his 'uniform' of a shirt and striped tie but when we see him at home he has a sense of style, for example, a stone-coloured textured overshirt with a t-shirt underneath, reminding us of Nadia's tendency to wear 'layers' and so perhaps giving a sartorial hint at their compatibility.

This case-study has shown how costume is an important signifier in films which would appear not to use it as spectacular display. Since *Wonderland* relates to the genre of social realism, costume is used to enhance its claim to represent something of 'the real'. It shows, for example, how people adapt clothes for their own ends, and can, like Nadia, be creative with inexpensive garments. Social and cultural verisimilitude is enhanced by the film's recognition that someone like Nadia would often wear similar clothes. We see her in several variations on the same basic style, the 'layered' approach with a preference for shirts with delicate patterns, made from thin materials so that they can reveal a little of an intriguing garment worn underneath. Her preference for hoods is also observed as we see her in two different jackets which are basically the same shape and style but made from different materials. This emphasis on similarity rather than difference contrasts with the other films which have been examined. In *Titanic*, *The Talented Mr Ripley* and *Desperately Seeking Susan,* the costumes depended to a much greater extent on a dynamic of difference, particularly in relation to their common concern to delineate class structures. In films like *Wonderland,* costume changes are far more subtle and gradations of style need to be carefully observed. Clothes are not used to create a spectacle in themselves but are used to support character and acting style. This is not, however, to argue that they are insignificant. As we have seen with Nadia, costume can also be used to suggest a character's complexity, an element of 'the self' which might not otherwise be apparent but which it is important for us to recognise in order to develop a more sophisticated understanding of her personality. In this sense it acquires the function of 'excess' which costumes often demonstrate as qualifying, or even contradictory, visual signifiers.

Also in contrast to the other films, *Wonderland* uses clothes which could be bought by anyone. The emphasis is on ordinary, everyday fashion garments such as t-shirts, leggings, jumpers and jackets. Meaning is not really mediated by stardom either since many of the actors in *Wonderland* were associated with the 'social problem' genre, the most well-known being Gina McKee who appeared in the television drama *Our Friends in the North* (1996). Apart a feature film role in *Human Traffic* (Justin Kerrigan, 1999) John Simms is best known as a television actor in *The Lakes* (1997), *Cracker* (1995) and *Clocking Off* (1999). This absence of external signifiers such as stardom allows the clothes in *Wonderland* to relate instead to themes which are important as meta-narrative, particularly the sense of place. The London locale is central to the film's depiction of one family's story over four days within a cityscape which is marked by a fractured and uncertain sense of time and space. The postmodern city is evident in Winterbottom's distinctive shots, described by Xan Brooks as 'his free-form mosaic of London life' (2000: 62), which suggest the timelessness of tube trains, of people walking the streets, of speeded-up cars, of people entering and leaving pubs and, from Nadia's high-rise flat, of London landmarks such as St Paul's Cathedral.

The four days in the life of the family are thus inserted within a much larger canvas which conveys the pace, fluidity and alienating space of modern city life. As in the mise-en-scène of other social realist films, clothes are therefore not just about individual bodies but reflective of social groupings and the negotiations which take place between 'the self' and the environment. As well as expressing character Nadia's clothes can be interpreted as expressive of postmodern uncertainty. The fact that we can identify her with a personal style which she has adapted from mass-produced clothing is an excellent example of 'lived practice', of how the same items can be worn differently in an attempt to express the self in a context of sameness, to both 'stand out' as an individual and 'fit in' with a group.

This approach to the city is not, of course, new to the social realist genre. As John Hill observed, it was a convention of the British 'New Wave' films of the 1960s to include shots of the landscape which were not necessarily related to the advancement of the narrative. The inclusion of what he terms 'realistic surplus' served two basic functions, to signify 'reality' but also to express a director's authorial voice (1986: 132). Similarly, in *Wonderland* the shots of Nadia and her sisters walking along the street, and their interspersion with the 'authorial' speeded-up or slowed-down shots of the cityscape, allows bodies and costumes to become part of Winterbottom's expression of the 'reality' of postmodern life. In contrast to *Desperately Seeking Susan*, in which the camera allows us to examine the costumes very precisely, especially in relation to their key role in the advancement of plot, Winterbottom's different aesthetic style both denies and permits such scrutiny. As noted previously, a dominant cinematographic strategy in *Wonderland* is the use of close-up. At times it is quite difficult to see what the characters are wearing, while on other occasions, when he places their bodies in communal situations, such as Nadia's 'wandering' sequences which are linked to his impressionistic shots of the city, or her meeting with Dan in a bar, they are very much in evidence. This has the effect of stitching the characters and their clothes into a much larger fabric, placing the individual in both intimate and more social spaces, and relating them outwards to a meta-narrative about urban living. *Wonderland* therefore uses costume as an integral marker of authenticity, of embodying elements of 'the real'.

5   THE MATRIX: FASHIONING THE FUTURE

Date: c. 2199
Place: simulated computer training program of the Matrix which like the Matrix creates the illusion of 1999
Location: crowded city street
Purpose: to train Neo, who has been brought back to his true self by the resistance movement led by Morpheus, to challenge the Matrix

The Matrix (Wachowski Bros., 1999) raises still more interesting issues regarding the role that costume plays in narrative development and character identification. Within the computer program, Neo (Keanu Reeves) walks with Morpheus (Laurence Fishburne) in the opposite direction from people who are dressed in black and white clothes, many of them wearing 'uniforms' as office workers, bankers, police, lawyers and sailors. Also present is a woman wearing a red dress, a classic *femme fatale* with blonde hair who stands out from the crowd and who causes Neo to turn his head as she walks past him in a languorous, seductive manner, momentarily distracting him and in so doing allowing himself to be aimed at by an Agent. After the program has been switched off, frozen in freeze-frame, Morpheus warns Neo against such lapses, of his need to be perpetually alert in the 'real' artificial world known as the Matrix.

The Matrix was created by Artificial Intelligence at the beginning of the twenty-first century to serve the needs of machines and is policed by Agents who wear dark suits and distinctive black shades. As Morpheus explains, the machines use bio-electricity from humans to survive, re-cycling humanity by liquefying the dead and feeding the residue back into a regeneration process. In the Matrix, humans are locked into the illusion of living in 1999 whereas the real, post-apocalyptic world which Morpheus and the other rebels roam in his ship/hovercraft, is a horrific and dangerous place with only one surviving human city, near to the earth's core, called Zion. The incident of the red dress occurs at a key moment in the film when Neo learns about the fictional status of the 'world' as he knew it, of which he was ignorant until rescued by Morpheus and Trinity (Carrie-Anne Moss), another member of the resistance. The woman in the red dress stands out as an alluring element of the Matrix, one of the pleasurable facets of an artificial world which both distracts and captivates its inhabitants. We learn that she was created for training purposes by Mouse (Matt Doran), one of the rebels on the ship; she is a creature of a male imagination which we also recognise as a classic representation of the feminine as a trap, as dangerous yet seductive. The colour red of course stands for sexuality and blonde hair is associated with the *femme fatale* of the film noir genre, a signifier of the perilous 'spider woman' who threatens and disturbs the male characters (see Kaplan 1980). As a simulation of the Matrix she is also indicative of its dangers, of how most of its inhabitants are unaware of their status as prisoners, as sources of battery power for machines.

The Matrix can be read as a critique of postmodernism. The world of the Matrix relates to what Jean Baudrillard (1998a) has identified as negative features of postmodern society, resulting in a media-saturated world in which originality is lost and accustomed significations are unbalanced as we are surrounded by floating images which come to stand in for 'the real'. They refer only to themselves, rather than the actual. Suggestive of this connection, early on in the film we see Neo remove a forbidden chip which he has procured in his capacity as a 'hacker' (someone who commits illegal computer crimes), from inside a copy of Baudrillard's *Simulacra and Simulation* (1994). Later, when Morpheus tells Neo about the Matrix he refers to the post-apocalyptic world as 'the desert of the real', a phrase used by Baudrillard in his discussion of simulation. Indeed, Baudrillard's notion of the 'hyperreal', defined as 'the generation by models of a real without origin or reality', would appear to describe the Matrix perfectly. As such the Matrix and the woman in red can be linked to a nightmare vision of postmodernity in which 'reality' is fiction. As Morpheus instructs Neo, the Matrix is 'the world that has been pulled over your eyes to blind you from the truth', the truth of being a slave born into 'a prison for your mind'. Yet the film unsettles because by contrast, the real world of c. 2199 is far from a utopian alternative, as articulated by the Judas-like character Cypher (Jon Pantoliano) who betrays the rebels after choosing to be re-inserted into the Matrix as a more comfortable and pleasurable option. Indeed, in its opposition to the Agents as representatives of Federal government, the resistance movement of c. 2199 embodies many of the elements associated with the anti-liberal philosophy of *survivalism**. Being aware of the Matrix and living as a member of the resistance under the authority of Morpheus is depicted as dangerous, ascetic and physically painful. The film by no means offers a safe, preferable alternative and is actually ambivalent in its critique of the Matrix.

The costumes in *The Matrix* are key indicators of the differences between the 'real' or 'hyperreal' (Matrix) and the real (post-apocalyptic life on Morpheus' hovercraft). They also underline the tension referred to above whereby the pleasures of postmodern society are pitted against the realities of a harsh future which, paradoxically, demonstrates the ideals of modernism – a belief in 'the truth'; faith in a Leader, Neo being presented as 'The One', the Saviour; clearly defined gender roles on the ship. As we shall see, an analysis of the costumes further problematises the film's critique of postmodernism as the 'residual self-image' is fashionable and alluring, inspiring imitation (tie-ins with manufacturers of 'Neo trenchcoats'; Airwalk footwear and dark shades designed by Blind Optics) and is associated with sexual transgression. The costumes, designed by Kym Barrett, display all the aesthetic credentials of postmodern fashion, 'its obsession with surface, novelty and style for style's sake' (Wilson 1985: 11). As reflective of fragmented identities and sensibilities, the fashions of The Matrix encourage performance, creativity and a de-stabilising of signifiers usually associated with particular garments. They also invite a discussion of fetishism and androgyny*, two key areas in relation to costume and cinema.

The central character played by Keanu Reeves has two identities from the start, as Thomas Anderson, computer programmer for 'a respectable software company' and as Neo, a 'hacker' who has explored the boundaries which have been placed around electronic communications. This split identity enables the rebels to single him out as someone who is curious about the Matrix but as yet unable to comprehend 'the truth'. This dual identity is visualised in the first shot of Neo when we see him head down, asleep in front of his computer with the patterns of its text reflected on his face. He wakes up when a message from Trinity appears on the screen. In the world of the Matrix before his 're-birth' on the rebel ship, he is dressed in black t-shirts or a dark suit at work, looking unremarkable. Once he is on the ship he undergoes a transformation in which his body is the object of spectacular display. The tantalising notion, that he might be 'the One' to save the last vestiges of humanity from being completely engulfed by the Matrix, introduces a further element of suspense as Neo's physical appearance changes in keeping with his elevation from computer programmer/hacker to potential Saviour.

The scenes of physical re-birth are of fundamental importance in making a distinction between body and costume. Neo re-gains his 'real self' by a cleansing process which is represented with violent birth imagery as his naked body is covered in a sticky, slimy substance, his head is shaved and he is propelled down a series of tubes in a mise-en-scène which is obtrusive in its organic form. We see his body undergo a painful metamorphosis, a rigorous rite of passage as it were, before he can learn the full truth about the Matrix. This sequence is important, since it exposes Neo's vulnerability that is later concealed by the costumes he wears when he is in the Matrix. Susan Jeffords argues that in the 1980s the male body was frequently displayed as muscled, hard and spectacular, whereas by the 1990s this had given way to 'a more internalised masculine dimension' that was less aggressive and more emotional (1993: 245). The scene of Neo's 're-birth' implies a rite of passage, a mode of preparation for the battles he is to fight to defeat the Matrix, wearing costumes that are a spectacular, if parodic, display of 'hard' masculinist imagery.

During the recovery period, Neo wears a grey sweatshirt which is in keeping with the scruffy, bland and rough clothes worn by the rest of the crew when they are on board the hovercraft. It is as if their bodies, rather than their clothes, are the primary sites of identity. We know that the cleansing process would have occurred with all those rebels who had been born in the Matrix, the implication being that their status as 'true' human beings is reflected in the purity of their 're-born' naked selves rather than in their costume. Neo's initiation into the resistance is therefore crucial in fixing his identity as 'the One' and in many ways his 'birth' attire is his most spectacular costume. It is significant that the clothes worn by the rebels on the ship are similar, functional and without regard for fashion. This is in keeping with John Flügel's ideas about *utopian dress**, that it should not distract or detract from the body: 'Complete reconciliation with the body would mean that the aesthetic variations, emendations and aggrandizements of the body that are produced by clothes would no longer be felt as necessary or desirable' (quoted in Wilson 1985: 219). As the only world that we see outside the Matrix, life on the ship represents an alternative to the Baudrillardian, postmodern nightmare described by Morpheus. In this reactionary scenario, clothes are accorded a negative status as fashionable and pleasurable markers of fragmented identities and sensibilities, suitable only for the hyperreality of the Matrix.

When Neo is undergoing his training and when he is re-inserted into the Matrix, his clothes are completely different from the utilitarian outfits he wears on the ship. When he is inside a computer training program with Morpheus he has a stylish haircut and sports a black straight-lined fashionable jacket. Similarly, Morpheus has a black suit, distinctive dark shades and a green tie. Both look like a feature from a contemporary men's fashion magazine. Indeed, there is an element of performativity and grandeur about Morpheus' costumes, particularly his long black trenchcoat with its leathery, reptilian textures. As John Harvey has observed in his study of the association between men and black clothing, dark attire has a double effect in relation to power: 'it steps outside, or sidesteps, the established grades of social class, while at the same time, by its gravity, it immediately creates its own dutiful-disciplinary élite' (1995: 238). This mobile feature of social stratification is an appropriate observation for Neo and Morpheus in their attempt to resist the dominant structures of the Matrix. In keeping with the film's play with cinematic genre, the coat is also reminiscent of those worn in westerns in which long coats conceal an armoury of weapons. Towards the end of the film when Neo rescues Morpheus from the Agents, he wears a similar coat (but made from wool) which at times looks like a fulsome cloak, complete with black shades and heavy boots. This stress on play and performance through costume – Neo is dressed for the part of the gun-blasting show-down – is associated with the hyperreal world. Yet it is also a considerable element of the film's visual pleasure which perhaps qualifies its ostensible critique of postmodern society. The shiny surfaces, the glamorous shades and tactile, leathery textures of the clothes are sensual, providing a language of panache and excess which is entirely absent from the ascetic regime of the ship.

There is perhaps a contradictory quality in Morpheus' attire which also qualifies the film's apparent endorsement of modernism over

Figure 8: Neo (Keanu Reeves) and Trinity (Carrie-Anne Moss), preparing for attack in *The Matrix*.

Figure 9: Morpheus (Laurence Fishburne) in *The Matrix*.

postmodernism. Although he is dressed spectacularly when he is in computer training programs or the Matrix, there are some disturbing similarities between aspects of his costume and that worn by the Agents. The Agents, particularly Agent Smith, wear dark grey/black suits with narrow, black ties and shades which resemble the clothes worn by CIA agents. The colour black has particular connotations, as Harvey has observed (257): 'alone or in the ranks, the man in black is the agent of a serious power'. Thus the similarity of attire worn by Morpheus and the Agents suggests that power is a constantly shifting mechanism. The shades in particular can be likened to those worn by Morpheus, especially in reflective shots which have sinister connotations. As Ruth Rubinstein has noted, 'mirrored lenses, the kind that make the wearer look like a state trooper, are most effective in turning back the looks of others' (1995: 253). When, for example, Morpheus asks Neo to choose between the red and the blue pill – to learn the truth about the Matrix or stay oblivious – we see his face reflected in Morpheus' shades in a shot which is reminiscent of the famous image of Marion Crane's nervous face reflected in the policeman's sunglasses in *Psycho* (Alfred Hitchcock, 1960), as she drives away from Phoenix after stealing money from her boss. The gravity of this moment of choice for Neo is therefore represented in an ambivalent manner by inserting an intertextual reference which perhaps casts doubt on Morpheus' motives. While the world of the Matrix is criticised by him for operating under strict controls and rules, the regime of the ship is no less hierarchical, and his insistence that Neo is 'the One' bears an uncomfortable resemblance to the worship of charismatic leaders in totalitarian societies. An accessory – the shades – has therefore suggested a more complex relationship between modernism and postmodernism, that there are connections and continuities between the two concepts. The dark trenchcoats, thick, heavy boots and shotgun armoury also suggest an uncomfortable allusion to fascist iconography. It is as if the rebels must out-class their enemies in their adoption of militaristic costume in the final shoot-out.

When contrasted with Morpheus' coat with its reptilian textures, Neo's woollen coat likens him to a lamb to the slaughter, continuing the Biblical allusion to him being identified as 'the One', the Saviour.

Elizabeth Wilson has argued that many themes and qualities identified with postmodernism have been evident in fashion for many centuries, particularly fashion's ability to transgress gender boundaries (1998: 400). *The Matrix* uses costume to play with issues of gender identity and androgyny, although this only occurs in the hyperreal world of the Matrix or in the computer programs which relay mental projections of the 'digital self'. It is noticeable that on the ship, gender boundaries are strictly binary and heterosexual. Trinity's clothes are ordinary and her hair is longer and softer than we have seen in the Matrix and she is cast in the role of handmaiden, quietly serving Neo his food and saving him at the end by declaring her love for him. This is in stark contrast to her black, shiny, body-hugging cat-suits and short, slicked-back androgynous haircut which typifies her appearance for most of the film when she is in the Matrix. The shiny material stands out like a suit of armour, revealing the contours of her body but also reflecting outwards. When she enters the battle with Neo to save Morhpeus she appears like a warrior, both of them glamorous in their spectacular black costumes.

The other great change is in the character Switch (Belinda McClory), whom we first see accompanying Trinity in a car when they fetch Neo to meet Morpheus. Switch has short blonde hair with a quiff, and there is an insinuation of lesbianism in her interactions with Trinity as she points a gun at Neo and treats him with far less deference than Morpheus who has singled him out as 'the One'. This attitude does not prevail on board ship. Switch's hair has a conventional cut and there is none of the sexual suggestiveness of the earlier scene. Again, we might conclude that it is the world of the Matrix that is more transgressive, more tolerant of difference than that which is typified by the resistance. The other major female character, the Oracle, in whom Morpheus has such faith, does nothing to disturb conventional representations. She is a mother-figure,

Figure 10: Trinity in *The Matrix*.

dressed in an apron and a flowery, patterned green dress and foresees the love-match between Neo and Trinity. As a possible dominant figure, her image as a sagacious but eccentric 'earth-mother' qualifies any momentous impact the Oracle might have had on the narrative.

The female costuming invites a discussion of fetishism, particularly in science-fiction films. Female attire is often masculinised or sexualised in films which are set in the future but with the contours of the body clearly visible, a classic example being Jane Fonda's 'space-age' outfits in *Barbarella* (Roger Vadim, 1968). Trinity's black shiny suits suggest a sexual, androgynous look which unsettles her more conventionally feminine persona on the ship; in a Freudian reading, however, her clothes are fetishistic, serving to allay male fears of castration in their sexual, phallic appearance (Wilson 1985: 95). This interpretation assumes that Trinity is 'read' in a male, heterosexual context. As Entwistle and others have pointed out, however, fetishistic clothing does not necessarily imply male creation or consumption (Entwistle 2000: 194; Bruzzi 1997: 37-8). Trinity's costumes both display and conceal her body, for example her shiny black outfit which exposes her shoulders and neck but covers the rest of her body in a tight PVC-type material. As mentioned above, this has the effect of reflecting back her image in a playful and erotic manner which exceeds castration anxiety. Although in terms of the narrative she is not a *femme fatale* or a woman to be feared by the male characters (it is, however, implied that she rejected Cypher's attentions), the tightness of her costume when she is in the Matrix is nevertheless suggestive of fetishistic pleasure through constriction.

In a discussion of tight-lacing and fetishism, David Kunzle (1982) has argued that tight clothing can be related, as it is here, to sexuality and to eroticism. Similarly, Neo's costumes are heavy, black and saturated with phallic imagery, including shotguns, wide silver-buckled belts and thick-soled black buckled boots. As a spectacular display of warrior-imagery they can be read as fetishistic but also, crucially, as a parody of masculinist imagery associated with regimentation, discipline and power (see Harvey 1995: 234-239). In terms of its representations of gender, the postmodern world of the Matrix has therefore proved to be a sophisticated site of play and self-reflexivity. In keeping with costume in the science-fiction film (see Jennsen 1987), the costumes in *The Matrix* are deliberately spectacular.

The Matrix also plays with generic traditions in a way which de-stabilises signifiers which are usually associated with particular garments. At the noir-ish beginning of the film, for example, a group of police burst in on Trinity in a dark room of a high-rise building. They wear uniforms which connote US police – peaked-caps, truncheons fastened to their belts – but the 'cops' are immediately juxtaposed with the Agents who reprimand them for not trapping Trinity when they arrive outside the building. Instead of looking rather shambolic, as detectives are usually coded in American crime dramas as they arrive on the scene of the crime, the Agents are superior in their sartorial precision, wearing dark suits, white shirts, narrow black ties with thin, silver tie-pins and the distinctive shades which have been previously mentioned.

Their suits are later contrasted with Neo's when he is working as Thomas Anderson: their superior status is signalled through their sharp suits which go with their powerful position. As the watchdogs of the Matrix, the Agents are dressed the same as each other but different from the rest. While a suit would normally suggest stability, authority or bureaucracy and a uniform would imply repression, the use of these garments in *The Matrix* has proposed a reversal of roles in the sense that the police are incompetent but despite their less elaborate or terrifying uniforms, the Agents are coded as the true holders of power. Like the CIA/FBI they are 'unseen' but nevertheless all-powerful. To underline this key difference the cynicism and bravado of Agent Smith is juxtaposed with the rather dim-witted remarks made by the police who underestimate Trinity's abilities. On a political level, this contrast relates to a conflict between federal and local power structures. The rebels thus represent a challenge to and resentment of federal authority.

As in many futuristic science-fiction films, *The Matrix* uses familiar technology but invests it with superior powers. The mobile telephone is a key accessory which reflects its current-day usage by guiding Neo to Trinity and Morpheus while the humble public telephone is the rebels' method of transference from the Matrix to the ship, from the 'hyperreal' to the 'real' world. Again, this is consistent with the film noir genre in which telephones are often an important accessory for plot development. But whereas in film noir they are accomplices to duplicity, double-crossing and mis-information, in *The Matrix* they are a lifeline (landline!) to our heroic protagonists who must subvert technology for their own ends, in Neo's case the computer and for Morpheus and the other rebels, computers and telephones. In view of the rebels' rather nostalgic yearning for past certainties, it is significant that older technology is elevated to a strategic status.

The use of costume in *The Matrix* is very much about spectacular display. This has an important narrative function in that spectacular garments convince us that the characters – Neo, Trinity and Morpheus – are capable of undermining the Matrix. Indeed, they must out-perform the Matrix in order to triumph. They have to be a sartorial match for the super-cool Agents whose dress is distinctive and connotive of power and knowledge. Clothes are therefore used in a classic way to empower characters by making them visually appealing. Yet this has consequences for the film's critique of postmodern society, since the costumes associated with the Matrix are attractive and compelling, a homage to style, performance and parody. The possibilities of computer-generated simulation are demonstrated to be far more pleasurable and, from the perspective of gender identities, progressive, than 'real' life as it is depicted on the ship. Here, the characters wear casual, light or insipid-coloured t-shirts and costume does not distract from the business of resistance. Of course it could be argued that in order to defeat the Matrix the rebels would have to be 'invisible' and therefore dress accordingly, but that still does not explain why their costumes are so remarkable, even for the purpose of 'training' programs. Austerity and the need for frugal living on the ship would explain the dull attire worn by the rebels but not their attitudes which would appear to be more conservative, particularly in terms of gender relations. Also, as I have argued, there is a convention in the literature of utopian dress that sees clothes as a problem, as a distraction from the fundamental site of importance – the body. In terms of the film's focus on Neo's re-birth and the sanctity of his naked body, it would therefore appear to endorse this view. On the other hand, as the image of the woman in the red dress shows, clothes not only distract but they also intrigue, impress and carry with them a range of signifiers which exceed their material existence. Thus, Neo cannot be 'the One' unless he *appears* to be 'the One'.

CONCLUSION

The previous chapters have suggested different approaches to film costume analysis and questions of characterization, plot development and thematic expression. It will be apparent that a careful study of the role of costume in a film's mise-en-scène illuminates the effect of specific choices made by the director and costume designer. Highlighting costume also extends beyond the text, in raising issues of authorship and the various factors that determine a film's overall 'look'.

In the case studies I have presented, it is evident that the directors had a clear conception of each film's particular style. The very different conceptions of realism held by both Baker (*A Night to Remember*) and Cameron (*Titanic*), for example, required contrasting usages of costume, in the former case blending in with the rest of the mise-en-scène, while in the latter departing from it in a more spectacular, 'excessive' manner. As we have seen, for the Wachowski brothers, the costumes for *The Matrix* are an integral aspect of the film's thematic address, as well as contributing a great deal to its exploration of ideas at a subtextual level.

Yet clearly the composition of film costume is not solely determined by the director. Collaboration with the costume designer is crucially important, as demonstrated by the work of Ann Roth in *The Talented Mr Ripley* and of Kym Barrett in *The Matrix*. Drawing on the director's overall conception of a film's 'look', the designer contributes a great deal to its realization and on occasion can augment, or even depart from that vision. Even with notoriously controlling directors such as Alfred Hitchcock, there is evidence of director-designer negotiation, in this case Edith Head's designs for many of Hitchcock's films. Her papers, from designs to memoranda, housed in the Margaret Herrick Library in Los Angeles, reveal the extent of her influence and can be studied as an example of the work of one of Hollywood's most prolific non-couturier designers. Detailed scrutiny of the designs and papers of particular designers has the potential therefore to destabilize the taken for granted authority of the director in envisaging a film's style. This can also be undertaken at a textual level, as Stella Bruzzi (1997) has shown in her analysis of Jean-Paul Gaultier's designs.

Another factor of key significance in determining a film's costuming is the persona of a particular actor or actress. As the cases of *Titanic* and *Desperately Seeking Susan* have shown, the respective identities of Di-Caprio and Madonna exerted an undoubted influence on the designs considered to be most appropriate for the characters. In these cases an overt address to the star's contemporary popularity and image was privileged over other factors. Casting can therefore act as a key determinant (or even constraint) on the range of designs feasible for a particular role. Paradoxically, in some cases designers can be more daring when working with actors and actresses who are less famous than the top stars whose images already have been formed. A certain homage to the intertextual persona of a star is therefore on occasion required. Some stars will use costume, however, in order to make a conscious break from their established image. Helena Bonham-Carter is a case in point, departing from her dominant image as an upper-class 'period lady' in British costume dramas such as *Howards End* (James Ivory, 1993), to playing the dishevelled Marla Singer in *Fight Club* (David Fincher, 1999), a contemporary American film.

As noted in the introduction, film costume has not been researched extensively in comparison with other areas of film studies. Yet its potential is immense. While this book has concentrated on questions of narrative, realism, gender identity and performance, there are many other areas which invite further investigation. These include different costume styles and traditions in various national cinemas. A specific cultural address will often be articulated in a film's style, and costume is no exception to this claim. Informed analyses of the costuming in, for example, Indian, Chinese or Japanese cinema contributes an insight into the construction and impact of a film's indigenous address.

Another potentially productive area is a consideration of costumes in television. With its assumed affinity to realism, the mise-en-scène of television drama has rarely been examined with the thoroughness of film analysis. Yet costumes are a key element of television dramas, soaps, sit-coms and even the news. Just as in film they are carefully chosen to create a particular effect, and some, particularly sci-fi series such as *Star Trek*, *Dr Who* and *Red Dwarf*, utilize spectacular costumes which become mythologized in popular memory. As the case study of *Wonderland* has shown, there are links between the style (reliance on close-up/'realistic' camera combined with highly stylised sequences) chosen by Michael Winterbottom and that utilized by many contemporary British television dramas. A similar approach to costuming as an attempt to convey 'the real' is also evident.

Yet another relatively unexplored area is the relationship between theatre and film costumes, particularly as far as early cinema is concerned when it is likely that there was considerable overlap. Charting when film costumes began to develop traits which were specifically appropriate to cinema rather than to the stage would produce a fascinating study. It is hoped that this book will encourage such further investigations as well as alerting ourselves to the function of costume in new films as they are released. As with *The Matrix* and the other films analysed in this book, the work of film costume continues to develop both its conventions and instances of spectacular intervention.

GLOSSARY

Definitions given here are related to the specific use of these terms in their place of appearance in the text.

Aide-mémoire
An aid to memory. Costume used to provoke a particular memory or association.

Androgyny
Clothes which are ambivalent in their gender address.

Authenticating role/process
Costumes used to provide evidence that research into a historical period has been conducted. The clothes convince the audience that they are an accurate representation of styles worn in the past.

Bohemianism
An affinity with the arts; unconventional habits and flamboyant tastes.

Bricolage
Postmodern term to describe an assemblage of styles; eclectic borrowings and conscious use of 'quotations'.

Camp
An exaggerated and parodic style or behaviour; destabilizes conventional meanings and associations and is linked with gay culture.

Commodity fetishism
Marxist term that proposes that when capitalist economies produce goods for mass consumption the labour that has gone into their production is not acknowledged.

The object acquires prime significance, obscuring the labour relations that were necessary for its production. Hence while Madonna might be a symbol of rebellion, she is nevertheless implicated in the capitalist exploitation of her image.

Couturier designs
Clothes created by fashion designers, identified by their own 'label' and generally more expensive than mass-produced clothes.

Déclassé
Indicates fallen social status.

Diaphanous material
Light and delicate, almost transparent material.

Diegetic and Non-Diegetic
Within the fiction; elements experienced/seen/heard by the characters as well as by the audience. As opposed to *non-Diegetic*, elements experienced/seen/heard only by the cinema audience.

Femme fatale
Evil or threatening woman associated with characters in the film noir genre.

Fetish/Fetishism
Clothes or objects used in a symbolic manner to allay male fears of castration in psychoanalytic theory. Also refers to sexual pleasure derived from wearing and/or seeing particular garments.

Heritage
Term associated with costume/historical dramas; identified with high production values and a quest for period authenticity.

Hitchcockian McGuffin
A plot device that propels the narrative but which facilitates the advancement of subtextual elements. The 'means' rather than the substance of a film narrative.

Identity
Refers to sense of self and allegiance to a particular gender, sexual preference, race, religion, class, country, etc.

Intertextuality
The relationship of one utterance, or texts, to another. This implies that no text is self-contained and needs to be understood in relation to the many 'intertexts' that constitute its structure. These can be novels, other films, paintings, ideas,

the persona of a particular star etc. While these intertexts may be consciously introduced by the screenwriter/director they can also be produced by audiences as the films they watch trigger individual and collective associations.

Jouissance
An extreme, unsettling experience of enjoyment, delight or jubilation.

Punk
Subculture associated with popular music of late 1970s and 1980s. An 'alternative' style identified by rebelliousness; de-stabilizing of conventional images and clothes.

Retro-film noir
Recent films which re-create elements of 'classic' 1940s film noir genre, often in a parodic manner.

Scopophilia
Pleasure in looking; a fascination with the human form.

Semiotic
The study of 'signs' (for example, clothing) and their associative, culturally-specific meanings.

Stereotypical costuming
Clothes used to signify clearly identifiable 'types' in a short-hand fashion, relying on dominant conceptions of a particular class or person.

Subcultural style
Clothes that offer alternative styles to the dominant culture, or which seek to subvert accepted meanings.

Suffragette movement
Nineteenth- and twentieth-century women's movement with the aim of winning the right to vote. This was achieved first in New Zealand in 1893; in Norway in 1907; in Britain in 1918 (for women over the age of 30); in the USA in 1920; in France in 1944; and in Switzerland not until 1971.

Survivalism
Extreme belief in the need to protect local groupings from the intrusion and power of central government. Communities form, live in hide-outs and arm/prepare themselves for a post-Apocalyptic future when most of civilization has been destroyed by some violent, natural or man-made threat.

Tie-ins
Commercial links between clothes manufacturers and products worn by actors on screen. Facilitates 'copying' of clothes worn by stars.

Utopian dress
Clothes worn in a future, ideal society.

Verisimilitude
Semblance of truth; the ways in which films seek to convince audiences that what they represent is 'true'/probable/believable in the terms of the fiction and according to accepted social/cultural standards.

BIBLIOGRAPHY

Baudrillard, J. (1994) *Simulacra and Simulation* (Trans. F. Glaser). Ann Arbor, MI: University of Michigan Press.

____ (1998) *Selected Writings*. Cambridge: Polity Press.

____ (1998a) 'The Precession of Simulacra' in J. Storey (ed.) *Cultural Theory and Popular Culture: A Reader*. London: Prentice Hall.

Beauvoir, S. de (1949) *The Second Sex*. London: Picador.

Belton, J. (ed) (2000) *Alfred Hitchcock's Rear Window*. New York: Cambridge University Press.

Berry, S. (2000) *Screen Style: Fashion and Femininity in 1930s Hollywood*. Minneapolis and London: University of Minnesota Press.

Brooks, X. (2000) review of *Wonderland* in *Sight and Sound*, 10, 1.

Bruzzi, S. (1997) *Undressing Cinema: Clothing and Identity in the Movies*. London: Routledge.

Bruzzi, S and P. Church Gibson (eds) (2000) *Fashion Cultures: Theories, Explorations and Analysis*. London: Routledge.

Butler, J. (1990) *Gender Trouble: Feminism and the Subversion of Identity*. London: Routledge.

Cameron, J. (1998) 'Foreword' in Marsh, E. W. (ed.) *James Cameron's Titanic*. London: Boxtree.

Chierichetti, D. (1976) *Hollywood Costume Design*. London: Studio Vista.

Church Gibson, P. (1998) 'Film Costume' in J. Hill and P. Church Gibson (eds) *The Oxford Guide to Film Studies*. Oxford: Oxford University Press.

Cook, P. (1996) *Fashioning the Nation: Costume and Identity in British Cinema*. London: British Film Institute.

Craik, J. (1994) *The Face of Fashion: Cultural Studies in Fashion*. London: Routledge.

Eckert, C. (1990) 'The Carole Lombard in Macy's Window' in J. Gaines and C. Herzog (eds) *Fabrications: Costume and the Female Body*. London: Routledge.

Engelmeier, R. and P. (eds) (1997) *Fashion In Film*. Munich and New York: Prestel.

Entwistle, J. (2000) *The Fashioned Body: Fashion, Dress and Modern Social Theory.* Cambridge: Polity Press.

Flügel, J. C. (1930) *The Psychology of Clothes.* London: The Hogarth Press.

Gaines, J. (1990) 'Costume and Narrative: How Dress Tells the Woman's Story' in J. Gaines and C. Herzog (eds) *Fabrications: Costume and the Female Body.* London: Routledge.

_____ (2000) 'On Wearing the Film: *Madam Satan (1930)*' in S. Bruzzi and P. Church Gibson (eds) *Fashion Cultures: Theories, Explorations and Analysis.* London: Routledge.

Gaines, J. and C. Herzog (eds.) (1990) *Fabrications: Costume and the Female Body.* London: Routledge.

Hallam, J. with M. Marshment (2000) *Realism and Popular Cinema.* Manchester: Manchester University Press.

Harper, S. (1994) *Picturing the Past: The Rise and Fall of the British Costume Film.* London: British Film Institute.

Harvey, J. (1995) *Men In Black.* London: Reaktion Books.

Hayward, S. (2000) *Cinema Studies: The Key Concepts.* London: Routledge.

Head, E. (1978) 'Dialogue on Film' in *American Film*, 3, 7, 36.

Hebdige, D. (1979) *Subculture: The Meaning of Style.* London: Methuen.

Herzog, C. (1990) '"Powder Puff"' Promotion: The Fashion Show-in-the-Film' in J. Gaines and C. Herzog (eds.) *Fabrications: Costume and the Female Body.* London: Routledge.

Highsmith, P. (1999; [1955]) *The Talented Mr Ripley.* London: Vintage.

Hill, J. (1986) *Sex, Class and Realism: British Cinema and Society, 1956-63.* London: British Film Institute.

Hill, J. and P. Church Gibson (eds) (1998) *The Oxford Guide to Film Studies.* Oxford: Oxford University Press.

Hodgkinson, W. (2000) 'The Stylish Mr Ripley' in *Guardian Guide*, 19-25 February.

Jeffords, S. (1989) *The Remasculinization of America.* Bloomington: Indiana University Press.

_____ (1993) 'Can Masculinity Be Terminated?' in S. Cohan and I. Rae Hark (eds) *Screening the Male: Exploring Masculinities in Hollywood Cinema.* London: Routledge.

Jennsen, E. (1987) 'Visions of the Future: Costume in Science Fiction Films' in E. Maeder, (ed.) *Hollywood and History: Costume Design in Film.* London: Thames and Hudson.

Kaplan, E. Ann (ed.) (1980) *Women in Film Noir.* London: British Film Institute.

Kaplan, E. Ann (1990) *Screen and Monitor: A Critical Investigation of Image Culture.* Taiwan: Fu Jen University.

_____ (1993) 'Madonna Politics: Perversion, Repression, or Subversion? Or Masks and/as Master-y' in C. Schwichtenberg (ed.) *The Madonna Connection: Representational Politics, Subcultural Identities, and Cultural Theory.* Oxford: Westview Press.

Kuhn, A. (1985) *The Power of the Image: Essays on Representation and Sexuality.* London: Routledge.

Kunzle, D. (1982) *Fashion and Fetishism: A Social History of the Corset, Tight-Lacing and other forms of Body-Sculpture in the West*. Towota, NJ: Rowan and Littlefield.

Lapsley, R. and M. Westlake (1988) *Film Theory: An Introduction*. Manchester: Manchester University Press.

Laver, J. (1969) *Modesty in Dress: An Inquiry into the Fundamentals of Fashion*. London: Heinemann.

Laver, J. (1969) *A Concise History of Costume*. London: Thames and Hudson.

Lehmann, U. (2000) 'Language of the PurSuit: Cary Grant's Clothes in Alfred Hitchcock's *North By Northwest*' in *Fashion Theory*, 'Masculinities' Special Issue, 4, 4.

Lord, P. (1956) *A Night to Remember*. New York: Bantam Books.

Lubin, D. M. (1999) *Titanic*. London: British Film Institute.

Marsh, E. W. (1998) *James Cameron's Titanic*. London: Boxtree.

MacCabe, C. (1974) 'Realism and the Cinema: Notes on some Brechtian Theses' in *Screen*, 15, 2.

Mendes, V. and A. de la Haye (1999) *Twentieth Century Fashion*. London: Thames and Hudson.

Minghella, A. (2000) interview in *American Cinematographer*, 81, 1.

Mulvey (1975) 'Visual Pleasure and Narrative Cinema' in *Screen*, 16, 3.

_____ (1998) 'New Wave' Interchanges: Céline and Julie and *Desperately Seeking Susan*' in G. Nowell-Smith and S. Ricci (eds.) *Hollywood and Europe: Economics, Culture, National Identity, 1945-95*. BFI: London.

Munich, A. and M. Spiegel (1999) 'Heart of the Ocean: Diamonds and Democratic Desire in Titanic' in K. S. Sander and G. Studlar (eds.) *Titanic: Anatomy of a Blockbuster*. New Brunswick, NJ and London: Rutgers.

Nash, M. and M. Lahti (1999) '"Almost Ashamed to Say I am One of Those Girls": *Titanic*, Leonardo DiCaprio and the Paradoxes of Girls' Fandom' in K. S. Sander and G. Studlar (eds.) *Titanic: Anatomy of a Blockbuster*. New Brunswick, New Jersey and London: Rutgers.

Neale, S. (2000) *Genre and Hollywood*. London: Routledge.

Nowell-Smith, G. and S. Ricci (eds) (1998) *Hollywood and Europe: Economics, Culture, National Identity, 1946-95*. London: British Film Institute.

O'Sullivan, C. (2000) review of *The Talented Mr Ripley* in *Sight and Sound*, 10, 3.

Rowbotham, S. (1997) *A Century of Women: The History of Women in Britain and the United States*. London: Viking/Penguin.

Rubinstein, R. (1995) *Dress Codes: Meanings and Messages in American Culture*. Oxford: Westview Press.

Sander, K. S. and G. Studlar (eds.) (1998) *Titanic: Anatomy of a Blockbuster*. New Brunswick, NJ and London: Rutgers.

Schwichtenberg, C. (1993) (ed.) *The Madonna Connection: Representational Politics, Subcultural Identities, and Cultural Theory*. Oxford: Westview Press.

Segal, L. (1990) *Slow Motion: Changing Masculinities, Changing Men*. New Brunswick, New Jersey: Rutgers University Press.

Simmel, G. (1904/1971) 'Fashion' in D. Levine (ed.) *On Individuality and Social Forms*. London: University of Chicago Press.

Spicer, A. (1997) 'Male Stars, Masculinity and British Cinema, 1945-60' in R. Murphy (ed.) *The British Cinema Book*. London: British Film Institute.

Stacey, J. (1988) 'Desperately Seeking Difference' in L. Gamman and M. Marshment (eds) *The Female Gaze: Women and Viewers of Popular Culture*. London: The Women's Press.

_____ (1994) *Star Gazing: Hollywood Cinema and Female Spectatorship*. London: Routledge.

Steele, V. (1985) *Fashion and Eroticism: Ideals of Feminine Beauty from the Victorian Age to the Jazz Age*. Oxford: Oxford University Press.

Straayer, C. (2001) 'The Telented Poststructuralist: Heteromasculinity, gay artifice, and class passing' in Lehman, P. (ed.), *Masculinity: Bodies, Movies, Culture*. London: Routledge.

Street, S. (1995) 'Hitchcockian Haberdashery' in *Hitchcock Annual 1995-1996*. Ohio: The Hitchcock Annual Corporation.

_____ (2000) '"The Dresses Had Told Me": Fashion and Femininity in *Rear Window* in J. Belton (ed) *Alfred Hitchcock's Rear Window*. New York: Cambridge University Press.

Tseëlon, E. (1992) 'Fashion and the Signification of Social Order' in *Semiotica*, 91 (1/2).

Turner, G. (1988) *Film as Social Practice*. London: Routledge.

Veblen, T. (1899) *The Theory of the Leisure Class: An Economic Study of Institutions*. New York: Mentor.

Voller, D. (1992) *Madonna: The Style Book*. London: Omnibus Press.

Wilson, E. (1985) *Adorned In Dreams: Fashion and Modernity*. London: Virago.

_____ (1998) 'Fashion and Postmodernism' in J. Storey (ed.) *Cultural Theory and Popular Culture: A Reader*. London: Prentice Hall.

THE SHORT CUTS SERIES

A comprehensive library of introductory texts covering the full spectrum of Film Studies, specifically designed for building an individually-styled library for all students and enthusiasts of cinema and popular culture.

"This series is tailor-made for a modular approach to film studies ... an indispensable tool for both lecturers and students"

Professor Paul Willemen, Napier University

01   THE HORROR GENRE
FROM BEELZEBUB TO BLAIR WITCH

Paul Wells

The inaugral book in the *Short Cuts* series is a comprehensive introduction to the history and key themes of the horror genre. The main issues and debates raised by horror, and the approaches and theories that have been applied to horror texts are all addressed. In charting the evolution of the horror film in social and cultural context, Paul Wells explores how it has reflected and commented upon particular historical periods, and asks how it may respond to the new millennium by citing recent innovations in the genre's development, such as the 'urban myth' narrative underpinning *Candyman* and *The Blair Witch Project*.

"An informed and highly readable account that is theoretically broad, benefiting from a wide range of cinematic examples"

Xavier Mendik, University College Northampton

ISBN 1-903364-00-0   144pp

02   THE STAR SYSTEM
HOLLYWOOD'S PRODUCTION OF POPULAR IDENTITIES

Paul McDonald

The Star System looks at the development and changing organization of the star system in the American film industry. Tracing the popularity of star performers from the early 'cinema of attractions' to the internet universe, Paul McDonald explores the ways in which Hollywood has made and sold its stars. Through focusing on particular historical periods, the key conditions influencing the star system in silent cinema, the studio era and the New Hollywood are discussed and illustrated by cases studies of Mary Pickford, Bette Davis, James Cagney, Julia Roberts, Tom Cruise, and Will Smith.

"A very good introduction to the topic filling an existing gap in the needs of researchers and students of the subject"

Roberta Pearson, University of Wales, Cardiff

ISBN 1-903364-02-7   144pp

03   SCIENCE FICTION CINEMA
FROM OUTERSPACE TO CYBERSPACE

Geoff King and Tanya Krzywinska

Science Fiction Cinema charts the dimensions of one of the most popular film genres. From lurid comic-book blockbusters to dark dystopian visions, science fiction is seen as both a powerful cultural barometer of our times and the product of particular industrial and commercial frameworks. The authors outline the major themes of the genre, from representations of the mad scientist and computer hacker to the relationship between science fiction and postmodernism, exploring issues such as the meaning of special effects and the influence of science fiction cinema on the entertainment media of the digital age.

"The best overview of English-language science-fiction cinema published to date ... thorough, clearly written and full of excellent examples. Highly recommended"

Steve Neale, Sheffield Hallam University

ISBN 1-903364-03-5   144pp

04 EARLY SOVIET CINEMA
INNOVATION, IDEOLOGY AND PROPAGANDA.

David Gillespie

Early Soviet Cinema examines the aesthetics of Soviet cinema during its 'golden age' of the 1920s, against a background of cultural ferment and the construction of a new socialist society. Separate chapters are devoted to the work of Sergei Eisenstein, Lev Kuleshov, Vsevolod Pudovkin, Dziga Vertov and Alexander Dovzhenko. Other major directors are also discussed at length. David Gillespie places primary focus on the text, with analysis concentrating on the artistic qualities, rather than the political implications, of each film. The result is not only a discussion of each director's contribution to the 'golden age' and to world cinema, but also an exploration of their own distinctive poetics.

"An excellent book ... Lively and informative, it fills a significant gap and deserves to be on reading lists wherever courses on Soviet cinema are run"

Graham Roberts, University of Surrey

ISBN 1-903364-04-3   144pp

05 READING HOLLYWOOD
SPACES AND MEANINGS IN AMERICAN FILM

Deborah Thomas

Reading Hollywood examines the treatment of space and narrative in a selection of classic films including *My Darling Clementine*, Its a *Wonderful Life* and *Vertigo*. Deborah Thomas employs a variety of arguments in exploring the reading of space and its meaning in Hollywood cinema, and film generally. Topics covered include the importance of space in defining genre (such as the necessity of an urban landscape for a gangster film to be a gangster film); the ambiguity of offscreen space and spectatorship (how an audience reads an unseen but inferred setting) and the use of spatially disruptive cinematic techniques such as flashback to construct meaning.

"Amongst the finest introductions to Hollywood in particular and Film Studies in general ... subtler, more complex, yet more readable than most of its rivals, many of which it will displace"

Professor Robin Wood, *Cineaction*

ISBN 1-903364-01-9   144pp

06 DISASTER MOVIES
THE CINEMA OF CATASTROPHE

Stephen Keane

Disaster Movies provides a comprehensive introduction to the history and development of the disaster genre. The 1950s sci-fi B-movies to high concept 1990s 'millennial movies', Stephen Keane looks at the ways in which the representation of disaster and its aftermath are borne out of both contextual considerations and the increasing commercial demands of contemporary Hollywood. Through detailed analyses of such films as *Airport*, *The Poseidon Adventure*, *Independence Day* and *Titanic*, the book explores the continual reworking of this, to-date, undervalued genre.

"Providing detailed consideration of key movies within their social and cultural context, this concise introduction serves its purpose well and should prove a useful teaching tool"

Nick Roddick

ISBN 1-903364-05-1   144pp

07 THE WESTERN GENRE
FROM LORDSBURG TO BIG WHISKEY

John Saunders

The Western Genre offers close readings of the definitive American film movement as represented by such leading exponents as John Ford, Howard Hawks and Sam Peckinpah. In his consideration of such iconic motifs as the Outlaw Hero and the *Lone Rider*, John Saunders traces the development of perennial aspects of the genre, its continuity and, importantly, its change. Representations of morality and masculinity are also foregrounded in consideration of the genres major stars John Wayne and Clint Eastwood, and the book includes a number of detailed analyses of such landmark films as *Shane, Rio Bravo*, *The Wild Bunch* and *Unforgiven*.

"A clear exposition of the major thematic currents of the genre providing attentive and illuminating reading of major examples"

Ed Buscombe, Editor of the BFI Companion to the Werstern

ISBN 1-903364-12-4   144pp

08 PSYCHOANALYSIS AND CINEMA
THE PLAY OF SHADOWS

Vicky Lebeau

Psychoanalysis and Cinema examines the long and uneven history of developments in modern art, science and technology that brought pychoanalysis and the cinema together towards the end of the nineteenth century. Vicky Lebeau explores the subsequent encounters between the two: the seductions of psychoanalysis and cinema as converging, though distinct, ways of talking about dream and desire, image and illusion, shock and sexuality. Beginning with Freud's encounter with the spectacle of hysteria on display in fin-de-siècle Paris, this study offers a detailed reading of the texts and concepts which generated the field of psychoanalytic film theory.

"A very lucid and subtle exploration of the reception of Freud's theories and their relation to psychoanalysis's contemporary developments - cinema and modernism. One of the best introduction to psychoanalytic film theory available"

Elizabeth Cowie, University of Kent

ISNB 1-903364-19-1   144pp

10 MISE-EN-SCENE
FILM STYLE AND INTERPRETATION

John Gibbs

Mise-en-scène explores and elucidates constructions of this fundamental concept in thinking about film. In uncovering the history of mise-en-scène within film criticism, and through the detailed exploration of scenes from films as *Imitation of Life* and *Lone Star*, John Gibbs makes the case for the importance of a sensitive understanding of film style, and provides an introduction to the skills of close reading. This book thus celebrates film-making and film criticism alive to the creative possibilities of visual style.

"Clearly written, helpful and accessible ... it tells a largely forgotten piece of the history of film criticism in Britain."

Ed Gallafent, University of Warwick

ISNB 1-903364-06-X   144pp